Son of Perdition: Uncovering the Antichrist

Andrew J. Lamont-Turner

Published by Andrew J. Lamont-Turner, 2024.

Table of Contents

Cover Page Image by https://pixabay.com/users/
sammy-sander-10634669/

Foreword

Exploring the intricate layers of this subject matter has proven to be a challenging endeavour as I crafted this book. Throughout the process, I grappled with the delicate balance of not amplifying the presence of evil beyond its warranted significance. However, amid this contemplation, I couldn't ignore the imperative significance of comprehending the Antichrist, as emphasized in Matthew 24:24, which warns that even the devout may fall prey to deception.

Hence, I persisted in penning this tome, driven by the conviction that understanding the eschatological figure of the Antichrist is paramount for navigating the complexities of the end times. The urgency to equip ourselves with discernment and knowledge becomes evident as it empowers us to stand unwavering amidst the tumultuous currents of these prophesied events.

It's important to note that this book represents a mere fraction of the exhaustive exploration warranted by such a profound topic. A wealth of additional texts is awaiting scrutiny, awaiting examination through the lens of Antichrist identity. As I embark on this journey of enlightenment, I pledge to refine and expand upon these insights in subsequent editions, striving to offer a more comprehensive understanding.

Through continued study and contemplation, I endeavour to deepen my comprehension and share newfound revelations with those interested in unravelling the Antichrist's mysteries. Thus, this book serves not as a final word but as a catalyst for ongoing dialogue and enlightenment in our quest for truth and discernment.

In Christ

Andrew

Chapter 1: Introduction

The references to the Antichrist in Scripture, particularly in the letters of John, paint a vivid picture of this enigmatic figure. The apostle John's writings highlight the essence of the Antichrist as one who opposes Christ, rejecting both the Father and the Son (1 John 2:22), denying the incarnation of Jesus (1 John 4:3), and refusing to acknowledge Jesus' coming in the flesh (2 John 1:7). John's admonition in 1 John 2:18 alerts believers to the presence of many antichrists in the world, foreshadowing the arrival of the ultimate Antichrist.

Throughout biblical prophecy and eschatological discourse, the Antichrist emerges as the epitome of opposition to Christ, representing the culmination of hostility toward God's purposes. Foretold to arise in the final hour, this figure will surpass all previous adversaries of Christ in his defiance and hostility. It's widely anticipated among scholars of Bible prophecy that this Antichrist will not only oppose Christ but also masquerade as the true Messiah, deceiving many with his charisma and false claims.

Numerous biblical passages offer insights into the nature and actions of the Antichrist, painting a comprehensive picture of his character and deeds:

- Daniel 7 Describes a powerful and arrogant ruler who oppresses the Jewish people and seeks to alter divine laws and times.

- Daniel 9 Foretells a leader who establishes a covenant with Israel but later breaks it, signalling a great tribulation period.

• Mark 13:14 References the "abomination of desolation," associated with the Antichrist's desecration of sacred spaces.

• 2 Thessalonians 2:1–12: Portrays the "man of lawlessness," who exalts himself above everything called God and deceives many with false signs and wonders.

• Revelation 6:2 Depicts a rider on a white horse, symbolizing the Antichrist's deceptive appearance of peace and authority.

These passages collectively form a mosaic of prophecies surrounding the Antichrist, outlining his rise to power, deceptive tactics, and ultimate confrontation with Christ and His followers. As believers engage in discernment and study of Scripture, they gain insight into the signs and events heralding the end times, preparing them to stand firm in the face of deception and persecution.

Revelation 13 vividly portrays the menacing figure of the first beast rising from the sea, symbolizing the Antichrist, who derives power from the dragon, Satan himself. This beast arrogantly utters blasphemous words and wages war against the saints, embodying the epitome of evil in the end times.

However, the narrative of Revelation offers hope amidst the darkness, foretelling the ultimate fate of the Antichrist and his accomplice, the false prophet. They are destined for eternal condemnation in the lake of fire, as depicted in Revelation 19:20 and 20:10, marking the end of their reign of terror.

The term "Antichrist" encapsulates the essence of the end-times false Messiah. This figure rises to global prominence with the intent to eradicate both Israel and the followers of Jesus Christ. Speculation abounds regarding the identity of the Antichrist, with various individuals from political, religious, and historical realms proposed as potential candidates. The list of conjectured figures is extensive and diverse, from Vladimir Putin to Prince William, Pope Francis to former Presidents Obama and Donald Trump.

Despite the fervent debates surrounding the Antichrist's origins and identity, the Bible remains silent on such specifics. However, biblical prophecy, particularly in Daniel and Revelation, provides clues regarding the Antichrist's rise to power. Some scholars suggest that he may have emerged from a ten-nation confederacy or a revived Roman empire, drawing insights from passages like Daniel 7:24-25 and Revelation 17:7.

Moreover, conjecture regarding the Antichrist's ethnicity, such as the presumption that he must be Jewish to claim Messianic authority, remains speculative, lacking biblical substantiation.

Nevertheless, amidst the uncertainty, Scripture offers reassurance that the Antichrist's true nature will be exposed in due time. Second, Thessalonians 2:3-4 warns against deception, affirming that the revelation of the "man of lawlessness" will precede the culmination of the end times. This figure will exalt himself above all that is considered divine, ultimately proclaiming himself as God—a blasphemous act that seals his fate of destruction.

As believers navigate the complexities of discerning the signs of the end times, they find solace in the certainty that God's truth will prevail. The schemes of the Antichrist will be thwarted by the sovereign hand of Almighty God.

Indeed, unveiling the Antichrist's identity is anticipated to be a profound astonishment for many. Throughout history, individuals have quickly attributed the title of Antichrist to various figures, from religious leaders to political tyrants. Yet, as evidenced by Martin

Luther's conviction regarding the pope of his time or the widespread belief during the 1940s that Adolf Hitler embodied the Antichrist, such assertions have proven to be erroneous.

It is prudent, therefore, to exercise caution against hasty speculation and instead focus on the teachings of Scripture concerning the Antichrist. Revelation 13:5-8 provides a chilling depiction of this malevolent figure, describing his mouth uttering great blasphemies against God and waging war against the saints. This passage underscores the Antichrist's temporary dominion over the earth, granting authority to exert his influence over people from every corner of the globe.

Moreover, Revelation foretells a scenario where the Antichrist will deceive many, compelling them to worship him instead of the true God. However, a crucial distinction remains: those whose names are inscribed in the Lamb's book of life, a symbolic representation of God's elect, will not succumb to his deception.

As believers navigate the complexities of discerning the signs of the end times, it is imperative to ground interpretations in the timeless truths of Scripture rather than succumbing to the allure of conjecture. The ultimate unveiling of the Antichrist will occur by God's sovereign plan. Until then, steadfast adherence to biblical teachings offers the surest guide through the tumultuous times ahead.

Chapter 2: Overview

The prevalence of false Messiahs throughout history has become a sobering reality for humanity. From individuals claiming to be Jesus Christ reincarnated to self-proclaimed deities manifesting in human form, the world has witnessed a myriad of imposters seeking to deceive and manipulate the masses. One such infamous figure is Jim Jones, whose tragic legacy is a stark reminder of the dangers of charismatic charlatans.

However, the existence of false Messiahs should come as no surprise to observant Christians, as warned by Jesus Himself. In Matthew 24:24, Jesus cautions that many false Christs will arise, leading multitudes astray—a prophecy that continues to unfold in contemporary times.

Delving into the biblical perspective on this phenomenon, 1 John 2:18 serves as a pivotal starting point. The apostle John, writing to believers, acknowledges the presence of numerous antichrists in his time, signalling the onset of the final hour. This declaration holds profound significance, affirming the imminent culmination of the age and the fulfilment of eschatological prophecies.

John's assertion that "these are the end times" and "it is the final hour" encapsulates the moment's urgency, resonating with believers across generations. Despite the passage of centuries, the truth contained within these words remains as relevant today as it was in the first century. John's awareness of the last hour underscores the pivotal significance of the Messiah's advent. This once-in-an-era event forever altered the course of human history.

Scripture corroborates this truth, emphasizing the uniqueness of Christ's incarnation and the divine timing of His arrival. In Matthew

21:37, Jesus' parable of the tenants illustrates God's singular sending of His Son, signalling the culmination of an era. Galatians 4:4 further reinforces this divine timing, highlighting the fullness of time when God sent forth His Son, born of a woman under the law.

As believers navigate the complexities of the present age, the words of Scripture serve as a beacon of truth amidst the sea of deception. The recognition of the final hour beckons us to vigilance, steadfast faith, and discernment of the signs heralding the return of our Lord and Savior, Jesus Christ.

The fullness of time, marking the culmination of history and the advent of Jesus Christ, holds profound significance in Christian theology. As the Scriptures attest, Jesus' arrival heralded a pivotal moment in human history, representing the long-awaited fulfilment of divine promises. The anticipation of the Messiah's coming was deeply ingrained in the Jewish consciousness, as evidenced by the apostles' inquiry about the restoration of the Kingdom to Israel in Acts 1:6. This expectation underscored the association of previous eras with the arrival of the Messiah, making Jesus' incarnation a watershed moment that forever changed the trajectory of humanity.

Yet, alongside the genuine Christ, John highlights the presence of counterfeit Christ—antichrists—who emerge to deceive and subvert the work of the true Messiah. In 1 John 2:18, John warns that "there are now many antichrists," indicating that the phenomenon is not confined to a singular individual but encompasses numerous imposters throughout history. The term "antichrist" in Greek, "antichristos," carries a dual connotation, signifying both opposition to Christ and the attempt to supplant Him.

Indeed, these antichrists manifest in various forms, ranging from overt adversaries of Christ to subtle imitations seeking to usurp His authority. They cunningly masquerade as representatives of Christ while harbouring hostility toward Him beneath the surface. Thus, "anti" conveys opposition and substitution—a deceptive portrayal of Christ designed to deceive and mislead.

John's sobering admonition reminds believers to remain vigilant against the subtle machinations of false Christs and antichrists. While the genuine Christ has come in the fullness of time, the presence of counterfeit Christ underscores the ongoing spiritual warfare waged against the kingdom of God. As disciples of Christ, we are called to discern the spirits and steadfastly uphold the truth amidst the proliferation of falsehoods, standing firm in our allegiance to the true and living Christ who reigns supreme over all creation.

AS RECORDED IN SCRIPTURE, the cautionary words of our Lord Jesus Christ resonate deeply with believers, urging vigilance against the proliferation of false Christs and pseudochrists. In Mark 13:6, Jesus forewarns imposters who will emerge, claiming to be the Christ and leading many astray—a sobering reminder of the deceptive tactics employed by those who seek to deceive even the elect.

Indeed, history bears witness to a succession of antichrists and pseudochrists. These individuals cunningly masquerade as representatives of Christ while harbouring ulterior motives. While some openly oppose Christ, others subtly seek to usurp His rightful place, exploiting signs and wonders to deceive the unsuspecting.

As we reflect on the biblical prophecies concerning the ultimate Antichrist, we are confronted with the sobering reality of Satan's orchestrated deception. In 2 Thessalonians 2:9-10, Paul warns of the Antichrist's arrival, empowered by Satan to perform miracles and lying wonders, ensnaring those who reject the truth in their pursuit of deception.

The parallels between past false Christs and the future Antichrist are a grim foreshadowing of the havoc that will be wrought upon the world when the final pseudochristas arise. Just as previous deceivers have manipulated and misled specific groups of people, the ultimate Antichrist will wield unparalleled influence, captivating the hearts and minds of the entire global populace.

In light of these prophetic warnings, believers are called to remain steadfast in the truth, anchored in the love of Christ and unwavering in their commitment to the gospel. As the world teeters on the brink of deception, may we cling to the truth of God's Word, discerning the spirits and standing firm against the enemy's schemes, knowing that, ultimately, the victory belongs to the Lord.

JOHN'S EMPHASIS ON the awareness of the impending arrival of the Antichrist among his audience underscores the continuity of prophetic teachings throughout Scripture. While the term "Antichrist" may be unique to John's writings in the New Testament, the concept of a malevolent figure opposing Christ has roots in the prophetic utterances of the Old Testament.

Indeed, the prophets of old, including Daniel, foretold the coming of a final Antichrist, providing specific descriptions that would later find fulfilment in the eschatological figure John refers to. Jesus Christ Himself spoke of the emergence of false Christ and the culmination of deception leading to the abomination of desolation and the tribulations of the end times. Through His teachings, Christ illuminated the reality of an ultimate embodiment of deceit and opposition to God's purposes.

Moreover, the apostles, including Paul, echoed these prophetic warnings, emphasizing the imminent arrival of the man of sin, the son of perdition, who would seek to deceive the world and lead humanity astray from the truth of Christ. These apostolic teachings, recorded in their epistles, further reinforced the urgency of vigilance and discernment among believers.

The overarching narrative of Scripture reveals a cosmic battle between God and Satan, with the ultimate goal of Satan being to thwart the redemptive work of Christ and assert his dominion over creation. However, the victory ultimately belongs to Christ, who will triumph over the forces of darkness and establish His reign as King of Kings and Lord of Lords.

In this grand cosmic drama, the role of the Antichrist serves as a focal point, representing the culmination of Satan's rebellion and the ultimate deception perpetrated against humanity. Yet, even in the face of such formidable opposition, believers find hope and assurance in the sovereignty of Christ, who will ultimately vanquish the adversary and restore all things according to God's perfect plan.

The biblical narrative of Genesis 6:1-4 offers a glimpse into the ancient cosmic conflict between God and Satan, illuminating the lengths to which the adversary has gone to subvert God's plans and thwart the coming of Christ. In this passage, we encounter a chilling account of fallen angels, the "sons of God," who rebelled against their heavenly abode and descended to earth.

These fallen beings, once celestial beings created by God, succumbed to the allure of rebellion and became hosts for demonic forces. Their descent from heaven marked a pivotal moment in human history, as they defied the divine order and indulged in illicit relations with human women. The resulting offspring of this unholy union was a grotesque hybrid of demon and human—a manifestation of the corruption and wickedness that pervaded the earth.

The implications of this union reverberate throughout Scripture, as both Jude and Peter reference this event in their writings. Jude warns of angels who abandoned their initial estate and are now kept in chains of darkness. At the same time, Peter speaks of the angels who sinned and were cast down to hell, awaiting judgment.

The depravity witnessed in the cities of Sodom and Gomorrah, characterized by their pursuit of "strange flesh," finds its roots in this ancient rebellion of angels and the corruption it wrought upon humanity. The ability of angels to assume human form further complicates the narrative, as they engage in relations with women, resulting in the birth of a demonic progeny.

While the specifics of this account may be shrouded in mystery, its significance lies in its portrayal of the lengths to which Satan will go to disrupt God's plans and undermine His purposes. From the ancient rebellion of fallen angels to the present-day schemes of the evil one, the cosmic battle between good and evil continues to unfold, ultimately culminating in the victory of Christ over all powers and principalities.

As believers, we are called to remain vigilant against the enemy's wiles, standing firm in our faith and trusting in the ultimate triumph of Christ, who has conquered sin and death. We will one day establish His reign of righteousness and peace upon the earth.

The intricate tapestry of biblical narratives reveals a relentless assault by Satan upon the Messianic line, a calculated effort to thwart the redemptive mission of Jesus Christ. From the ancient corruption of humanity in Genesis to the attempted annihilation of Israel's descendants in Exodus and beyond, Satan's schemes have sought to disrupt God's plan of salvation and eradicate the hope of redemption.

In Genesis, Satan's diabolical plan unfolds as fallen angels engage in illicit relations with human women, resulting in the birth of a demonic progeny that he hoped would be beyond the reach of redemption by Jesus Christ. This corruption of humanity prompted God to send the flood, cleansing the earth of its wickedness and preserving a remnant through Noah's family.

Throughout history, Satan's assaults on the Messianic line persist, as seen in his attempts to slaughter Israel's descendants in Exodus, Jehoram's massacre of his brothers in II Chronicles, and the repeated attacks on the royal line, reducing it to a precarious thread time and again. Yet, despite Satan's relentless efforts, God's providential hand preserves the Messianic line through miraculous interventions and the faithfulness of His chosen servants.

Even in the face of mortal wounds and near-death experiences, such as those endured by Aziah, the lone survivor of the Messianic line, God's sovereign purpose prevails. Aziah's survival, though hanging by a thread, serves as a testament to God's unwavering commitment to His redemptive plan, ensuring that the lineage of the Messiah endures despite the onslaught of adversity and evil.

Ultimately, these narratives underscore the profound significance of the Messianic lineage and the relentless opposition it faces from the forces of darkness. Yet, in trials and tribulations, God's faithfulness remains steadfast, guiding and preserving His chosen people until the fulfilment of His promises in the advent of Jesus Christ, the ultimate Redeemer and Savior of humanity.

The relentless onslaught of Satan against the Messianic line and the redemptive mission of Jesus Christ is evident throughout Scripture, spanning from the Old Testament to the New Testament and continuing to the present day. From the cunning plots of rulers and adversaries to direct confrontations with the forces of darkness, Satan's attempts to derail God's plan of salvation are relentless and multifaceted.

In II Chronicles 22, the young Josiah stands as the sole survivor of the Messianic line, threatened by the schemes of evil forces seeking to extinguish the lineage from which the promised Messiah would arise. The book of Esther depicts Satan's insidious plot to annihilate the Jewish people, targeting the descendants of Abraham and thwarting God's covenant promises.

In the New Testament, Herod's attempt to slaughter all male infants in Bethlehem reflects Satan's desperate bid to eliminate the newborn King, Jesus Christ, before His ministry could begin. Later, in Matthew 4, Satan confronts Jesus in the wilderness, seeking to seduce Him away from His divine mission and divert His attention from the path of the Cross.

Even among Jesus' disciples, Satan's influence is evident, as seen in Peter's attempt to dissuade Jesus from embracing His sacrificial mission—a moment that prompts Jesus to rebuke him, declaring, "Get behind me, Satan."

The climax of Satan's opposition unfolds at the crucifixion, where he orchestrates a concerted effort to thwart Jesus' redemptive work, from the nails driven into His hands and feet to the spear thrust into His side. Yet, despite Satan's relentless attacks, Jesus triumphs over sin and death through His resurrection, securing victory for all who believe in Him.

Throughout history, Satan persists in his efforts to undermine Christ and deceive humanity, deploying a parade of false messiahs and counterfeit Christ to lead astray those who are not rooted in the truth. Yet, in the face of such opposition, the hope of redemption remains steadfast, anchored in the unwavering love and faithfulness of Jesus Christ, who reigns victorious over all powers and principalities.

The cosmic battle between good and evil, as depicted in Revelation 12, reaches its climactic moment during the time of the Tribulation—a period of intense upheaval and turmoil foretold in biblical prophecy. In this apocalyptic vision, war erupts in the heavens between the archangel Michael, his angelic hosts, the dragon identified as Satan, and his legions of fallen angels. This celestial conflict underscores the ongoing spiritual warfare that rages between the forces of light and darkness, with the fate of humanity hanging in the balance.

As Revelation 12 vividly portrays, the defeat of Satan and his cohorts results in their expulsion from heaven, casting them down to the earth. This pivotal event marks the true beginning of the Tribulation—a period of unparalleled chaos and suffering that will engulf the world in its grip. With the demonic forces unleashed upon the earth, humanity finds itself plunged into a nightmare scenario as the pit of hell is opened, releasing hordes of chained demons to wreak havoc and devastation upon the earth.

Amidst this cataclysmic upheaval, a figure emerges as the orchestrator of chaos and destruction—the Antichrist of Revelation 13. This individual, wielding unprecedented worldly power and authority, becomes the focal point of human allegiance and allegiance during this dark hour of history. His reign of terror and deception marks the zenith of the Tribulation, as he manipulates events on the world stage to further his diabolical agenda.

John's admonition to his readers, "You have heard that Antichrist shall come," serves as a sobering reminder of the pervasive awareness of this future figure, not only among Christians but also among pagans and cultures throughout history. The anticipation of an ultimate clash between good and evil, a final showdown between the forces of light and darkness, echoes across diverse religious and mythological traditions, pointing to a universal recognition of the cosmic struggle between righteousness and wickedness.

As the events of Revelation unfold, the true nature of this spiritual warfare becomes unmistakably clear as humanity is confronted with the stark reality of its own vulnerability and the relentless onslaught of evil forces. Yet, amidst the darkness and despair, there remains a glimmer of hope—a hope anchored in the promise of Christ's return and the ultimate triumph of good over evil, of light over darkness, ushering in a new era of peace and righteousness for all who place their trust in Him.

The ancient Babylonian creation myth featuring the primordial sea monster Tiamat and the hero Marduk bears intriguing parallels to biblical narratives, particularly in Isaiah's prophetic declarations regarding the defeat of Leviathan, the crooked serpent, and the sea monster. In both accounts, there is a cosmic battle between forces of good and evil, with the ultimate triumph of the divine over the chaotic forces of darkness.

In addressing the Babylonian mythological narrative, Isaiah uses it as a backdrop to assert the supremacy of the Lord over all creation. By referencing the Babylonian imagery of the final battle between Marduk and Tiamat, Isaiah communicates a powerful message of divine sovereignty and victory. He reassures his audience that just as the Lord conquered Leviathan and the sea monster in the mythological tale, He will prevail over all the forces of evil in the world.

Moreover, Isaiah's prophetic utterances regarding the defeat of Leviathan and the sea monster serve as a reminder of God's sovereignty over the entire cosmos, including the spiritual realm. By depicting God as the ultimate victor in the cosmic struggle against evil, Isaiah instils hope and confidence in his audience, assuring them that God's power and authority are unmatched and His purposes will ultimately prevail.

In addition to biblical narratives, historical figures such as Antiochus Epiphanes serve as foreshadows or prototypes of the eventual Antichrist, as described in the book of Daniel. Daniel's use of the term "Antichrist" concerning Antiochus underscores the complex interplay between biblical prophecy and historical events, highlighting the ongoing struggle between the forces of light and darkness throughout history.

The convergence of mythological motifs, biblical prophecy, and historical events underscores the universal significance of the cosmic battle between good and evil. Whether portrayed through ancient myths or biblical narratives, the overarching theme remains the same: the ultimate triumph of God over all the forces of darkness and the fulfilment of His divine purposes in the world.

The historical figure of Antiochus Epiphanes serves as a chilling precursor to the Antichrist described in Revelation 13. Like many tyrants throughout history, Antiochus sought to eradicate Judaism and suppress the worship of the one true God. His ruthless campaign included barbaric acts such as outlawing circumcision, desecrating the Temple in Jerusalem with pagan rituals, and persecuting those who adhered to the Jewish faith. His reign of terror was fueled by a diabolical desire to eliminate any hope of a Messiah arising from the Jewish people.

Yet, as history and prophecy converge, Antiochus Epiphanes is but a foreshadowing of the ultimate Antichrist, whose rise to power will unleash unparalleled chaos and devastation upon the earth. In Revelation 13, this malevolent figure is depicted as a mirror image of Christ, wielding authority and influence over the nations during a time of great tribulation. As demonic forces swarm the earth and God's wrath is poured out upon the wicked, the Antichrist stands at the epicentre of this global cataclysm, exuding a magnetic charisma that draws multitudes to his side.

Revelation 13 unveils five key aspects of the Antichrist's reign: his imposing presence, his apparent injury and miraculous recovery, his blasphemous claims of divinity, his relentless pursuit of conquest and dominance, and his ominous warnings of judgment upon those who oppose him. As the world hurtles towards the brink of destruction, the Antichrist emerges as a figure of unprecedented power and influence, orchestrating events with chilling precision as he seeks to establish his dominion over all of humanity.

Yet, even amidst the darkness and chaos of the Tribulation, there remains hope for those who stand firm in their faith and refuse to bow to the Antichrist's tyranny. The ultimate victory belongs to God, who will one day vanquish the forces of evil and usher in a new era of peace and righteousness for all who trust Him.

The grandness of the Antichrist

The vivid imagery portrayed in Revelation 13 unveils the emergence of a fearsome figure known as the Beast, a key figure in the prophetic narrative of the Antichrist. John, the visionary author, stands on the sea's shore and witnesses the Beast ascending from the tumultuous waters, symbolizing the rise of this malevolent force from the masses of humanity.

The Beast is described with ten horns and seven heads, adorned with blasphemous names and crowned with authority. Its appearance is likened to a leopard, with feet reminiscent of a bear and a mouth akin to a lion. This imagery echoes the prophetic visions of Daniel, who foresaw similar beasts arising from the sea, each representing different kingdoms and powers.

The fatal wound inflicted upon one of the Beast's heads, miraculously healed to the world's amazement, further adds to this enigmatic figure's mystique. The Beast is endowed with great power and authority, granted by the dragon, identified elsewhere in Revelation as Satan himself. As the world marvels at the Beast's might, they are deceived into worshipping both the Beast and the dragon, acknowledging their supremacy over all earthly dominions.

The Beast's reign is characterized by blasphemy against God and persecution of the saints, wielding authority over every tribe, people, language, and nation. Despite the tribulations believers endure, John emphasizes the need for endurance and faith in adversity.

Drawing parallels to Daniel's vision, the Beast rising from the sea symbolizes the emergence of a Gentile ruler from among the nations. The sea, representing the masses of humanity, serves as the backdrop for the Beast's ascent to power, suggesting that he will arise from within the tumultuous currents of human history, likely from the Mediterranean region.

As the prophetic narrative unfolds, the identity and actions of the Beast serve as a chilling reminder of the ongoing spiritual battle between good and evil, culminating in the ultimate showdown between the forces of darkness and the sovereignty of God.

The imagery of the Beast rising from the tumultuous sea, adorned with seven heads and ten horns, resonates deeply with symbolic significance, each representing a facet of political authority and sovereignty. In the prophetic narrative of Revelation, these symbols offer insights into the nature and identity of the final global ruler, the Antichrist.

The Beast's seven heads and ten horns are laden with metaphorical meaning, indicative of immense power, authority, and dominion. Historically associated with strength, the horns symbolize the potent force wielded by the ruler. Meanwhile, the crowns atop the horns signify dominance and control, further accentuating the ruler's sovereignty over the nations.

A deeper understanding of these symbols can be gleaned from Revelation 17, where the Beast is depicted with seven heads and ten horns adorned with blasphemous names. This intricate imagery reveals a pattern that unveils the ultimate form of the Antichrist's global dominion. In verse 9 of Revelation 17, the seven heads represent seven mountains, traditionally associated with Rome, often referred to as the "seven-hilled city."

The correlation between the seven heads and the seven mountains upon which the woman (symbolizing worldly powers and systems) sits suggests a connection to Rome as the epicentre of the Antichrist's reign. This association hints at a convergence of political, religious, and global authority centred in Rome, serving as the focal point of the Antichrist's power and influence.

Thus, the imagery of the Beast with seven heads and ten horns is a compelling depiction of the Antichrist's unparalleled authority and dominance over the nations, with Rome potentially emerging as the nexus of his global dominion.

Indeed, the intricate symbolism in Revelation 17 unveils a complex narrative, where the false religious system of mystery Babylon is depicted riding upon the Beast, suggesting a symbiotic relationship between political and religious powers. Rome emerges as a focal point, given its significant religious influence on the world at the time.

Verse 10 offers further insights into the nature of the Beast's authority, portraying the seven heads as representative of geographical mountains and seven monarchs or rulers. Five have fallen, one is present, and another is yet to come, indicating a succession of great world empires throughout history. Many interpreters identify these empires as ancient civilizations such as Greece, Persia, Assyria, Babylon, and Egypt, with the Roman Empire existing at the time of John's writing. The final ruler, symbolized by the eighth head, is believed to be associated with the resurrected Roman Empire, suggesting a continuation or revival of its dominion.

This interpretation aligns with the prophetic insights of Daniel, who also foretold the rise and fall of successive world empires. The Roman Empire, as the sixth head, holds a pivotal role in this sequence, with the seventh head representing its resurgence. Contemporary events, such as the expansion of the European economic community and the formation of the Common Market, where nations territorially overlap with the historical boundaries of the Roman Empire, offer intriguing parallels to this prophetic narrative.

Daniel's prophecies indeed provide crucial insights into the trajectory of global powers, particularly regarding the resurgence of the Roman Empire. In Daniel chapters 2 and 7, the imagery of the statue with ten toes and the ten horns on the fourth beast signifies a confederacy or alliance composed of ten entities. This confederacy is widely interpreted as representing the final form of global authority, characterized by the revived Roman Empire.

The potential for the resurrection of the Roman Empire is evident in contemporary geopolitical dynamics, including discussions surrounding European integration, the formation of a European army, and political manoeuvring within the European Union. These developments align with the prophetic narrative of a confederacy emerging from the territories once governed by Rome.

Verse 10 in Daniel, when read alongside Revelation 17, offers a comprehensive view of this final form of global authority. The symbolism of the seven heads, representing successive world empires, culminates in the resurrected Roman Empire, which embodies the characteristics of its predecessors while surpassing them in strength and dominance. This revived empire, led by the ten kings or horns, represents a formidable force unparalleled in human history.

The emergence of this empire, marked by political consolidation and military prowess, sets the stage for the arrival of the Antichrist, who will wield unprecedented power and authority over the earth. The convergence of biblical prophecy with contemporary geopolitical trends underscores the significance of these ancient texts in understanding the future trajectory of global governance.

Indeed, the imagery presented in Revelation 13, particularly regarding the Beast emerging from the sea with seven heads and ten horns, provides significant symbolism regarding the nature and scope of this final global authority. The seven heads represent the culmination of all previous world empires. At the same time, the ten horns signify a confederacy of nations under the rule of the Beast.

The possibility of this confederacy centred around the European economic union or the Common Market aligns with the prophetic narrative of a revived Roman Empire exerting dominance over the earth. The brief duration mentioned in Verse 12 underscores the transient nature of this global authority, highlighting its temporary existence before the ultimate defeat by the Lamb, who is depicted as the Lord of Lords and King of Kings.

The presence of the label "Blasphemy" on the heads symbolizes the Beast's antagonistic stance against God and Christ, indicating its defiance and rebellion against divine authority. This blasphemous opposition is a defining characteristic of the final world power, showcasing its intent to challenge and oppose the sovereignty of the Creator.

In essence, the imagery portrayed in Revelation 13 vividly portrays the geopolitical and spiritual forces at play in the end times. It underscores the ultimate triumph of righteousness over evil and the sovereignty of Christ over all earthly powers, providing hope and reassurance to believers amidst the tumultuous events prophesied to unfold.

Indeed, the vision of this individual ruling the world is imposing and thought-provoking. The portrayal of the Antichrist as a distinct individual, rather than merely a system or ideology, is a consistent theme throughout Scripture, emphasizing the personal nature of this future figure.

Daniel's prophecies provide insight into the character and abilities of the Antichrist. Described as an intellectual genius with impressive oratory skills, he possesses a sharp intellect and persuasive tongue, enabling him to captivate and manipulate the masses. His ability to enter peacefully and gain power through flattery underscores his political cunning and strategic acumen.

Moreover, the Antichrist is depicted as a commercial genius, capable of establishing a global economic community and wielding significant influence over the world's financial systems. His mastery of commerce and economics further solidifies his grip on power and control.

Additionally, the Antichrist is characterized as a worshipper of military might, indicating his prowess in strategic warfare and military tactics. His command of military forces enhances his authority and enables him to assert dominance on a global scale.

Overall, the multifaceted portrayal of the Antichrist as an intellectual, political, economic, and military genius underscores the magnitude of his influence and the formidable challenges posed by his reign. As such, the warnings and prophecies concerning the Antichrist serve as a sobering reminder of the spiritual and geopolitical battles that lie ahead in the eschatological narrative.

The descriptions of the Antichrist in 2 Thessalonians 2:4 and Daniel paint a vivid picture of a figure who rebels against God, exalts himself above all, and possesses remarkable charisma and cunning. Referred to as a "man of sin" and a "son of perdition," he embodies intellectual prowess and spiritual deception, leading many astray with his persuasive rhetoric and false miracles.

Daniel's prophecy highlights the Antichrist's understanding of riddles and his connection to the spiritual realm, suggesting a dark power source beyond human capabilities. His rise to power is marked by cunning deceit and destructive conquests as he seeks to dominate and subjugate both nations and individuals. Despite his worldly success, his ultimate downfall is prophesied by divine intervention, underscoring the inevitable defeat of evil by the hand of God.

Furthermore, Daniel foretells the Antichrist's blasphemous arrogance and rejection of traditional gods, instead honouring a god of fortresses with lavish offerings. This defiance and self-aggrandizement signify his desire for absolute control and worship as he seeks to establish his divine authority over all creation.

In essence, the biblical descriptions of the Antichrist paint a chilling portrait of a charismatic yet malevolent figure who seeks to usurp God's authority and establish his own reign of terror and deception. As humanity navigates the complexities of the modern world, these prophecies serve as a sobering reminder of the spiritual warfare and moral challenges that lie ahead.

The illustriousness of the Antichrist

The imagery in Revelation 13:2, drawing parallels to Daniel's prophecies, offers a profound insight into the nature and characteristics of the Antichrist. Each element symbolizes a different aspect of his persona and reign, providing a comprehensive understanding of his power and influence.

The comparison to a leopard signifies swiftness, suggesting the rapid and agile manner in which the Antichrist will assert his authority and enact his plans. This denotes his ability to easily manoeuvre through political and societal landscapes, swiftly implementing his agenda and consolidating power.

Likewise, the reference to a bear highlights strength, indicating the Antichrist's formidable military prowess and ability to exert force to achieve his objectives. This strength may manifest in various forms, including military conquests, coercive tactics, and oppressive rule over nations and peoples.

Furthermore, the depiction of a lion's mouth symbolizes ferocity and tenacity, emphasizing the Antichrist's ruthless determination and relentless pursuit of dominance. His words and actions will be marked by boldness and aggression, instilling fear and awe in those who oppose him.

Moreover, the dragon's attribution of power, throne, and authority to the Beast underscores the spiritual dimension of his rule, indicating his alignment with Satan and his empowerment by demonic forces. This supernatural backing amplifies the Antichrist's influence and enables him to control vast realms and populations.

Regarding the mortal wound mentioned in verse 3, while some speculate about its significance and potential connection to resurrection, it is essential to interpret this symbolically rather than literally. The partial healing of the wound and the marvel it elicits from the world suggest a deceptive display of power and invincibility orchestrated by the Antichrist, aimed at furthering his agenda and solidifying his reign.

The interpretation of the wounded head of the Beast in Revelation 13 as a symbol of the resurrected Roman Empire holds significance in understanding the broader context of biblical prophecy and eschatology. While there are various interpretations of this imagery, the notion of the Beast representing a revived form of a historical empire aligns with certain thematic elements found throughout scripture.

In this perspective, the wounded head symbolizes the decline and fall of the Roman Empire, which historically experienced significant upheaval and fragmentation. However, the subsequent healing of this wound signifies the resurgence and restoration of imperial power as the world witnesses the reemergence of a dominant and formidable force akin to the ancient Roman Empire.

The world's marvel and astonishment at this revival underscores the magnitude of this event and its implications for global governance and geopolitics. The resurrection of such a powerful entity evokes awe and reverence, captivating the imagination of nations and individuals alike.

Moreover, linking this imagery to the concept of the Beast as a symbol of worldly authority and dominance reinforces the idea of human institutions and systems being subject to divine intervention and manipulation. The Beast's resurrection is a testament to the intricate interplay between human history and divine providence, illustrating how God's sovereign plan unfolds through the rise and fall of empires and kingdoms.

Ultimately, interpreting the wounded head and its healing as emblematic of the revived Roman Empire invites reflection on the cyclical nature of history and the enduring relevance of biblical prophecy in illuminating contemporary events and phenomena. As believers discern the signs of the times, they are called to remain vigilant and faithful, trusting in God's ultimate victory over the forces of darkness and the establishment of His eternal kingdom.

The worship of the Antichrist

The depiction of the Beast being worshipped in Revelation 13 reveals the extent of his influence and authority over the earth's inhabitants. The act of worship towards the Beast is not merely a sign of admiration or reverence. Still, it represents a profound submission to Satanic deception and manipulation. It is an expression of allegiance to the forces of darkness and a rejection of God's sovereignty.

The question posed by those who worship the Beast, "Who is like the beast? Who can make war with him?" reflects the perception of invincibility and supremacy attributed to the Beast. In the eyes of his followers, he embodies unparalleled power and authority, surpassing any earthly ruler or military force. This perception is reinforced by the acknowledgement that the dragon, symbolizing Satan, has bestowed his authority upon the Beast, elevating him to a position of unrivalled dominance.

Indeed, the Antichrist represents Satan's ultimate deception, a masterful embodiment of worldly prowess and charisma. Unlike historical figures such as Mussolini, Hitler, or Stalin, who pale in comparison to the Antichrist's allure and influence, the Beast emerges as the epitome of human achievement and leadership, captivating the hearts and minds of the masses.

The notion that most of the world's population, excluding those whose names are written in the Lamb's Book of Life, will worship the Beast underscores the depth of spiritual deception and apostasy that characterizes the end times. Despite evangelistic efforts and divine interventions during the Tribulation, many will succumb to the allure of the Beast's false promises and deceptive rhetoric.

The covenant between Israel and the Beast, as described in Daniel 9:26-27, further highlights the depth of deception and betrayal that will unfold during the Tribulation period. Israel's willingness to enter into a covenant with the Beast, believing him to be the Messiah, exposes the extent of spiritual blindness and delusion that permeates society at that time.

In essence, the worship of the Beast signifies humanity's collective rejection of God's truth and submission to the forces of evil. It serves as a stark reminder of the consequences of forsaking divine guidance and succumbing to the allure of worldly power and deception.

The concept of believers whose names are inscribed in the Lamb's Book of Life before the foundation of the world serves as a profound source of comfort and assurance amidst the tumultuous events described in the book of Revelation. It highlights God's divine foreknowledge and predestination, ensuring that those who belong to Him will be safeguarded and preserved through even the most difficult circumstances.

As depicted in Revelation, the mark of the Beast symbolizes allegiance and conformity to the Antichrist's system of control and manipulation. Those who receive the mark on their forehead or hand demonstrate their willingness to submit to the Beast's authority and participate in his deceptive schemes. Conversely, those who refuse the mark face exclusion from societal participation, unable to engage in essential transactions such as buying or selling.

The emergence of a "number society," where transactions and interactions are governed by digital systems and technological advancements, foreshadows the potential implementation of a system of control akin to that of the Antichrist described in Revelation. The pervasive influence of technology in modern society raises questions about privacy, autonomy, and individual freedom, highlighting the relevance and prophetic significance of biblical warnings regarding the mark of the Beast.

In essence, the mark of the Beast serves as a stark reminder of the spiritual and ethical implications of allegiance and obedience. It prompts believers to remain vigilant and steadfast in their faith, resisting the allure of worldly power and conformity to systems that oppose God's truth and righteousness. Amidst the challenges and uncertainties of the end times, the assurance of salvation and divine protection for those whose names are written in the Lamb's Book of Life provides hope and strength to persevere in the face of adversity.

The warfare of the Antichrist

The portrayal of the Beast in Revelation depicts a figure of immense arrogance and audacity, characterized by a mouth that utters great boasts and blasphemies against God. This aligns with the prophetic descriptions provided in the book of Daniel, highlighting the continuity and consistency of Satan's character as he seeks to defame the name of God and undermine His authority.

The Beast's reign, specified as forty-two months or three and a half years, corresponds to the latter half of the seven-year Tribulation period. During this time, the Antichrist's blasphemous rhetoric intensifies, targeting not only God Himself but also His holy sanctuary and the faithful believers who dwell in heaven.

The prevalence of blasphemy throughout Revelation underscores Satan's overarching strategy to deceive and mislead humanity, particularly during times of great tribulation and upheaval. As catastrophic events unfold during the Tribulation, many people succumb to the Beast's deceitful tactics, blaspheming God in defiance and rebellion.

Furthermore, the Beast's authority extends beyond mere rhetoric, as he is granted the power to wage war against the saints and exert dominion over people from all nations and languages. This tyrannical rule culminates in the persecution and massacre of believers as the Beast ruthlessly suppresses any opposition to his reign.

The image of the Beast described as possessing the ability to speak and command obedience from the masses, symbolizes the pervasive influence and idolatrous worship that characterize his reign. Despite the horrors unleashed during this period, the Beast succeeds in deceiving and subjugating vast swathes of humanity, demonstrating the extent of his power and manipulation.

In essence, the depiction of the Beast's warfare and blasphemy in Revelation serves as a chilling reminder of the spiritual battle between good and evil, highlighting the insidious tactics employed by Satan to deceive and destroy those who oppose him. Yet, amidst the darkness and chaos, the steadfast faith of the saints ultimately prevails, as they remain faithful to God despite the immense pressure and persecution they face.

Indeed, the unfolding of evil and chaos during the Tribulation period serves a profound purpose in God's ultimate plan for redemption and restoration. While allowing evil to have its momentary reign, God is working behind the scenes to bring about the defeat of Satan's oppressive regime and the establishment of His eternal kingdom of righteousness and peace.

The martyrdom of saints and the persecution of believers during this tumultuous time may seem like a temporary victory for evil. Still, it is ultimately a testament to the unwavering faith and steadfastness of those who remain loyal to God, even in the face of adversity. As Daniel prophesied, while some saints may be worn down by the Antichrist's relentless onslaught, some will overcome and persevere through their faith in God.

The scene described in Revelation 15:2-3 provides a glimpse of the triumphant vindication of God's faithful servants. Those who overcome the Beast, his image, and the mark of his name stand victorious on a sea of glass mixed with fire, praising God for His righteous and marvellous works. This imagery symbolizes the ultimate victory of good over evil, righteousness over wickedness, and the establishment of God's eternal kingdom.

While the tribulations and trials of the end times may be harrowing and intense, they ultimately purify and refine the faith of God's people, preparing them to reign with Him in glory for all eternity. Thus, even in darkness and despair, the hope and assurance of God's ultimate victory shine brightly, inspiring believers to persevere and remain steadfast in their devotion to Him.

Indeed, the vision of the sea of glass mixed with fire in Revelation symbolizes the divine purity and holiness of God's presence, contrasting starkly with the turmoil and chaos of the earthly realm. It serves as a reminder that despite the trials and tribulations believers face, there is ultimately a place of perfect peace and restoration awaiting them in the presence of God.

The promise of a new Heaven and Earth, as described in Revelation, underscores the hope of a future where righteousness reigns, and every tear is wiped away. It signifies the culmination of God's redemptive plan, where His people will dwell with Him in eternal harmony and joy.

Amidst the challenges posed by the Beast and his reign of terror, the ultimate triumph of the saints is assured. Their unwavering faith and perseverance in the face of persecution will be rewarded as they stand victorious alongside their Savior in the glorious culmination of history.

As the warnings regarding the Beast's magnificence, wound, adoration, and battle resound throughout Revelation, they serve as a call to vigilance and steadfastness for believers. They remind us to remain faithful to God, even in adversity, knowing that our ultimate victory is assured through Christ.

The warning of the Antichrist

Verse 9's call, "If anyone has an ear, let him hear," indeed resonates with all humanity, urging each individual to heed the message and choose their allegiance. It is a universal invitation to consider the implications of aligning with the Antichrist's system or Christ's Kingdom.

In Revelation 13:10, the endurance and faith of the saints are emphasized, highlighting the unwavering perseverance of those who remain steadfast in their commitment to Christ. This endurance is not merely a passive acceptance of circumstances but a resolute determination to hold fast to their faith despite the trials and tribulations they may face.

The verse also speaks to the principle of retribution, indicating that those who perpetrate violence and oppression will ultimately face the consequences of their actions. Just as captors may become captives, and those who wield the sword may ultimately fall by it, divine justice ensures that every good or evil deed will be accounted for.

For believers, this understanding provides a source of hope and confidence, knowing that God's justice will ultimately prevail and His faithful followers will be vindicated. It underscores the importance of remaining steadfast in faith and trusting in God's ultimate sovereignty, even in the face of adversity and persecution.

Therefore, the call to "hear" and the reminder of the saints' endurance and faith serve as a beacon of hope and encouragement for all who follow Christ, reminding them that their ultimate victory is assured through Him.

Indeed, the self-destructive nature of evil is a fundamental principle highlighted throughout Scripture, offering assurance to believers that those who align themselves with the Antichrist's system are destined for failure. This understanding strengthens the patience and trust of the saints, knowing that the very nature of evil ensures its eventual downfall.

While the Antichrist is a specific individual who will emerge at the culmination of human history, it's crucial to recognize that the spirit of antichrist has existed in the world since ancient times. This spirit opposes Christ and His teachings, seeking to deceive and lead people from the truth.

In the subsequent chapter, we will delve deeper into the distinction between antichrists—those who embody the spirit of opposition to Christ—and the ultimate Antichrist, whose arrival heralds the culmination of evil's efforts to deceive and destroy. Understanding this distinction is vital for discerning the signs of the times and remaining steadfast in faith amidst the challenges posed by the spirit of antichrist.

Chapter 3: Antichrist vs antichrists

In 1 John 4:2–3, the term "antichrist's spirit" is introduced within the context of discerning spiritual influences. In writing to his audience, John addresses the prevalent worldview of his time, which was characterized by many spiritual beliefs, doctrines, and teachings. Various spirits claimed to offer truth and enlightenment in this diverse spiritual landscape, creating a confusing maze of ideas.

John provides a clear directive to navigate this complexity: believers should exercise discernment and test the spirits to determine their origin. He emphasizes the importance of discerning whether a spirit acknowledges Jesus Christ's incarnation, as those spirits aligned with God will affirm this fundamental truth. Conversely, any spirit that denies Jesus' true nature is not from God but embodies the spirit of the antichrist.

John's admonition underscores the presence of false prophets and deceptive teachings in the world, urging believers to remain vigilant and discerning in their spiritual discernment. In a world where numerous perspectives on truth abound, John's guidance is a timeless principle for distinguishing genuine spiritual influences from those opposing Christ's truth.

John's criteria for discerning spirits emphasizes the theological aspect, focusing on whether a teacher's doctrine aligns with the truth about Jesus Christ. Acknowledging Jesus Christ's incarnation—the belief that Jesus, as both fully divine and fully human, appeared in the flesh—is a foundational test of spiritual authenticity.

In John's context, this test directly addressed the rise of Gnosticism. This belief system denied the true humanity of Jesus Christ. Gnostics claimed that Jesus only appeared to have a physical body, leading to a rejection of His true humanity. By affirming Jesus Christ's genuine incarnation, believers could identify teachings inspired by the Holy Spirit and discern falsehoods propagated by deceptive spirits.

This theological test serves as a litmus test for discerning true spiritual guidance. Teachers and prophets who affirm the reality of Jesus Christ's bodily presence on earth align with God's truth. Conversely, those who deny or distort this essential truth propagate doctrines that oppose God's revelation.

Thus, John's guidance underscores the importance of sound doctrine in spiritual discernment and emphasizes the foundational truth of Jesus Christ's incarnation as a fundamental criterion for distinguishing between true and false spiritual influences.

Indeed, the antichrist's spirit stands in opposition to the truth of Jesus Christ, seeking to deceive and lead people away from Him. This spirit operates through individuals who deny or distort the fundamental truths about Jesus as revealed in the Bible. Those who reject Jesus Christ's divine nature, His incarnation, or His role as Savior fall under the influence of this deceptive spirit.

Throughout Scripture, the antichrist's spirit is depicted as a force of darkness and deception, seeking to obscure the light of the gospel and lead people astray. It is likened to birds snatching away the seeds of truth before they can take root, blinding unbelievers to the glory of Christ and perpetuating lies about His identity.

The apostle John warns believers to be discerning and vigilant against this spirit of deception, recognizing that it operates through false teachers and deceivers who deny Jesus Christ's true nature and mission. By remaining grounded in the truth of God's Word and the testimony of Jesus, believers can guard against the influence of the antichrist's spirit and hold fast to genuine faith in Christ.

Indeed, the Bible foretells the emergence of a global dictator known as "the beast" in the book of Revelation. This individual, empowered by Satan himself, will wield tremendous authority and demand worship from all. Described as having a mouth that speaks proud and blasphemous words, this figure represents the epitome of lawlessness and rebellion against God.

In 2 Thessalonians 2:3, he is referred to as "the man of lawlessness," destined for destruction. This final Antichrist will embody all the deceit and distortion of truth propagated by the antichrist spirit throughout history. Even now, the secret power of lawlessness is at work, sowing confusion and opposing the truth of Jesus Christ.

However, despite the influence of the antichrist spirit, believers are assured of victory through the indwelling Spirit of truth. As 1 John 4:4 declares, "You, dear children, are from God and have overcome them because the one who is in you is greater than the one who is in the world." This assurance reminds Christians that they are equipped to stand firm against the forces of darkness and falsehood, relying on the power of God within them to overcome any opposition.

Discerning is crucial in distinguishing between the spirit of the antichrist and the genuine Spirit of God. As outlined in 1 John 4:5–6, false prophets and those influenced by the antichrist's spirit operate from a worldly perspective, espousing ideologies that align with the values of the world. Consequently, they often gain widespread acceptance and influence among worldly-minded individuals. On the other hand, those who truly know God and are indwelt by His Spirit will recognize and adhere to the teachings of Christ and His apostles, even if these teachings are unpopular or contrary to worldly norms.

Testing the spirits involves careful examination and discernment, as emphasized in 1 John 4:1. Jesus Himself instructed His disciples to be shrewd as serpents and innocent as doves, highlighting the importance of cautious discernment (Matthew 10:16). Rather than blindly accepting teachings based on the reputation or credentials of the speaker, believers are called to evaluate the content of the message, particularly its Christology—what it professes about Jesus Christ.

In a world filled with diverse spiritual teachings and ideologies, it is imperative for believers to remain grounded in the truth of God's Word and to approach all teachings with discernment and wisdom, guided by the Spirit of truth.

Chapter 4: The Antichrist in Revelation

Revelation 13:1–10 unveils prophetic insights into the future global governance during a pivotal three-and-a-half-year period leading up to the return of Christ. This chapter delves into the key figures of the end times, including Israel, the dragon representing Satan, Christ, and Satan himself. Additionally, it introduces the significant personalities who will wield authority during the great tribulation: the beast, symbolizing the world ruler, and the false prophet, who will serve as the beast's religious collaborator throughout this tumultuous period.

The chapter commences with a scene where the dragon observes the emergence of the world ruler "from the sea." Although interpretations differ regarding whether John himself stood on the seashore or if it was a separate passage, the essence of the vision remains unchanged. John describes witnessing a beast rising from the sea, adorned with ten horns and seven heads, each crowned with blasphemous names. This beast resembles a leopard but possesses attributes reminiscent of a bear and a lion. Notably, the dragon bestows authority, power, and a throne upon the beast (vv. 1–2).

The beast's identity in Revelation symbolizes the resurrected Roman Empire and its ruler during the end times, a concept echoed in various passages across both Daniel and Revelation. In Daniel 7:7–8 and Revelation 12:3, the beast's imagery emerges, while Revelations 17:3 and 17:7 offer further insights into its significance.

The depiction of the beast emerging from the sea in Revelation parallels the imagery presented in Daniel 7:7–8, where the sea symbolizes the multitude of peoples and nations. This suggests that the future global dictator, embodied by the beast, will arise from a Mediterranean context, indicating the geographical region of the resurrected Roman Empire.

Furthermore, mentioning the ten horns on the beast signifies the ten governments or kingdoms that comprise this empire, a symbolism consistent with the political authority represented by horns in Daniel 7–8. The crowns adorning these horns denote governmental power, and their blasphemous names reflect their antagonism towards God.

The interpretation of the seven heads varies among scholars, with some associating them with previous eras of governance and others linking them to influential powers within these future governments. Nonetheless, the overarching symbolism portrays a formidable entity, representing the culmination of political and spiritual opposition to God during the end times.

Indeed, the imagery of the beast in Revelation 13:2, resembling a leopard with the feet of a bear and the mouth of a lion, draws parallels to the prophetic visions described in Daniel 7. In Daniel's vision, the lion represents the Babylonian Empire, the bear symbolizes the Medo-Persian Empire, and the leopard signifies the conquests of Alexander the Great and the subsequent Greek Empire. However, the specific beast described in Revelation 13:1–7, which combines elements of these earlier empires, represents the future Roman Empire.

The Roman Empire, often regarded as the fourth global empire in Daniel's prophecies, holds significant historical and prophetic importance. It emerged as a dominant force following the decline of the Greek Empire. It exerted considerable influence over the known world during its existence. The Roman Empire's impact on subsequent civilizations and its longevity as a global power solidifies its position as a key player in biblical prophecy.

The symbolism of the beast embodying characteristics from these earlier empires underscores its significance as the culmination of worldly power and authority. It suggests that the final world ruler will wield unprecedented influence, drawing upon the strengths and territories of past empires. Ultimately, as prophesied in Scripture, this ruler will ascend to a position of global supremacy, achieving a level of dominion unparalleled in history.

Indeed, the description of the beast receiving power and authority from the dragon, identified as Satan, underscores the spiritual dimension behind the end-time governmental regime. This portrayal aligns with the broader biblical narrative depicting Satan as the ultimate adversary of God and His purposes. In Revelation 12, the dragon is explicitly identified as Satan, the ancient serpent, who opposes God and seeks to thwart His plans.

The imagery of the beast's apparent fatal wound and subsequent healing has sparked considerable debate among interpreters. Some interpret this as a literal resurrection or miraculous recovery. In contrast, others view it symbolically, representing the revival or resurgence of the political authority represented by the beast. Regardless of the interpretation, the world's reaction to this event is significant. The astonishment and adoration expressed toward the beast illustrate its profound influence and power over humanity.

The worship of the beast and the dragon reflects humanity's alignment with and allegiance to the forces of evil. This worship starkly contrasts the worship and devotion owed to God alone. The rhetorical question posed— "Who is like the beast?"— highlights the perceived invincibility and superiority of the beast, further reinforcing its status as a symbol of worldly power and authority.

Overall, the depiction of the beast in Revelation 13 serves as a sobering reminder of the spiritual battle between good and evil, symbolizing the pinnacle of human rebellion against God and His kingdom.

Indeed, the interpretation of the beast's apparent fatal wound and subsequent healing is subject to various viewpoints and interpretations. While some have proposed literal resurrections of historical figures or individuals from the past to fulfil this role, such as Judas Iscariot or historical tyrants like Nero, Mussolini, Hitler, or Stalin, these explanations face challenges in reconciling the vast array of potential candidates and the theological implications of such resurrections.

An alternative interpretation, gaining traction among scholars, is to view the fatal wound not as pertaining to a specific individual but rather to the empire or political entity symbolized by the beast. In this view, the resurrection of the beast represents the resurgence or revival of the Roman Empire, which, despite its historical demise, experiences a renewed manifestation or influence in the end times.

This interpretation aligns with the broader thematic framework of Revelation, which often employs symbolic language and imagery to convey spiritual truths and prophetic insights. The idea of a seemingly defeated or extinct power experiencing a revival or resurgence is a common motif in apocalyptic literature, underscoring the cyclical nature of historical empires and the enduring influence of worldly powers throughout human history.

Ultimately, the precise understanding of the beast's fatal wound and subsequent healing remains a matter of interpretation. Scholars continue to debate robustly and discuss its significance within the broader context of Revelation's eschatological vision.

Another scenario offers an intriguing perspective on the nature and significance of the beast's fatal wound and subsequent healing. The notion of an assassination attempt against the world ruler, followed by a miraculous healing orchestrated by Satan, underscores the supernatural dimension of this end-time figure's authority and power. It highlights the allure and awe-inspiring abilities that draw people to worship the ruler and the malevolent force behind him.

The worship of the beast and Satan represents the ultimate form of apostasy and rebellion against God, as it involves placing human and demonic entities above the divine. This echoes the ancient desire of Satan to usurp God's authority and be worshipped as a deity (Isaiah 14:14). The worship of the beast symbolizes humanity's rejection of God's sovereignty and submission to earthly powers and spiritual deception.

Moreover, your reference to the prophetic passages in Ezekiel 38-39 adds depth to the discussion, suggesting a potential alignment with geopolitical events and biblical prophecy. The envisioned scenario of a major conflict involving Russia and its allies invading Israel, only to face divine intervention and defeat, resonates with the themes of divine judgment and the ultimate triumph of God's sovereignty over the nations.

As with all interpretations of eschatological prophecy, these perspectives invite further reflection and exploration, stimulating ongoing dialogue and inquiry into the mysteries of God's unfolding plan for humanity's ultimate redemption and restoration.

The duration of the beast's reign, depicted as forty-two months or three and a half years, aligns with various prophetic timelines found throughout Scripture, particularly concerning the period leading up to Christ's second coming. During this time, the beast exercises his authority with audacity, using his position to utter blasphemous words against God and slander His name, His dwelling place, and even the heavenly beings (Revelation 13:5-6).

The scope of the beast's dominion is staggering, as he is granted authority to wage war against and conquer the saints, demonstrating his power over all tribes, peoples, languages, and nations (Revelation 13:7). This global governance fulfils the prophecy in Daniel, which foretold the rise of a final global ruler who would exert dominion over the entire earth (Daniel 7:23). Throughout his reign, the beast's authority extends to the persecution and martyrdom of believers, as described in Revelation 7:9–17.

Moreover, the beast's rule is characterized by widespread worship, as all inhabitants of the earth who are not recorded in the Lamb's book of life worship him (Revelation 13:8). This universal adoration underscores the beast's deceptive allure and the extent of his influence over humanity, as he is elevated to a status akin to that of a divine being.

In essence, the portrayal of the beast's governance in Revelation highlights the culmination of human rebellion against God, as embodied by the ultimate ruler who blasphemes God, oppresses His people, and asserts authority over the entire world. However, it also serves as a reminder of the ultimate triumph of God's sovereignty and the eventual defeat of evil at the coming of Christ.

The Book of Life, referenced throughout Revelation, holds a pivotal role in understanding the ultimate fate of individuals in the context of the end times. While Revelation 13:8 suggests that all inhabitants of the earth, apart from those whose names are inscribed in the Book of Life, will worship the beast, the interpretation of this verse has sparked considerable debate among scholars and theologians.

One point of contention revolves around translating the phrase "from the foundation of the world." While some interpretations suggest that this phrase refers to the Lamb being slaughtered before the world's creation, others argue that it pertains to the Book of Life itself, indicating that names were recorded therein since its inception. This distinction has significant implications for understanding the nature and purpose of the Book of Life.

The function of the Book of Life, as described in Revelation 3:5, is believed by some to ensure the eternal security of the saved, guaranteeing that their names will not be erased. Some view the Book of Life as a registry for the saved, recording their names upon salvation. Others interpret it as a record of all living beings, with names inscribed until the point of death. At this time, they are either retained or removed based on their eternal destiny.

Furthermore, Revelation 22:19 alludes to the Tree of Life rather than the Book of Life, adding another layer of complexity to the interpretation. However, the overarching theme of eternal security throughout Scripture suggests that once an individual is saved, they are saved forever, shedding light on the meaning of Revelation 13:8. Consequently, those who are lost will worship the beast. In contrast, those who are saved will remain steadfast in their devotion to God.

While the exact interpretation of Revelation 13:8 may remain debatable, the broader theological principle of eternal security underscores the assurance of salvation for believers whose names are inscribed in the Book of Life.

The concluding verses of Revelation 13 echo a familiar refrain found throughout the letters to the seven churches: "He who has an ear, let him hear." This call to attentiveness underscores the importance of individual response to the gospel message. It highlights God's sovereignty in determining the outcomes of human actions. The passage acknowledges that some will be taken captive and others slain with a sword, emphasizing the need for Christians to demonstrate patience and fidelity amidst adversity (Revelation 13:9–10).

This invitation to heed the message is a recurring theme in Scripture, extending beyond the book of Revelation to various passages in the Gospels and other New Testament writings. It underscores each individual's responsibility to respond to God's call and align their lives with His purposes. While the focus of the call in Revelation 2–3 is directed towards the churches, in this context, it addresses individuals, suggesting that the church has already been raptured. Despite the potential for persecution and martyrdom, believers find comfort in the assurance that genuine faith in God will ultimately lead to everlasting bliss in His presence.

Furthermore, the passage emphasizes the inevitability of divine judgment for those who persist in evil and rebellion against God. While the full realization of justice may not be immediate, believers are encouraged to exercise patience and perseverance, trusting in God's sovereign plan for their lives and the world.

Revelation 13 paints a vivid picture of a future global government under the rule of a Middle Eastern king who will assert dominance over ten nations before establishing himself as the dictator of the entire world in the final three and a half years leading up to Christ's second coming. The events described in this passage support the belief that believers who have been promised deliverance from God's wrath will be raptured before the onset of this period, ensuring their protection and ultimate salvation in Christ.

Chapter 5: Antichrist and the church

The belief in the pre-tribulation rapture of believers in Jesus Christ is a prominent interpretation among many Christians, based on passages like First Thessalonians 4:13–18. According to this interpretation, the sequence of events at the rapture involves the resurrection of the dead in Christ, followed by the living believers being caught up to meet the Lord in the air. This event marks the conclusion of the church era, and believers are said to be united with the Lord forever.

Following the rapture, the seven-year tribulation period, as predicted in Daniel and Revelation, is believed to commence. During this time, a figure known as the Antichrist, or the beast, is described in Revelation 13 as exercising authority for forty-two months, symbolizing the second half of the tribulation. The defeat of the Antichrist is foretold in Revelation 19, coinciding with the second coming of Jesus Christ.

According to this interpretation, believers living in the church era will not witness the emergence of the Antichrist because they will be raptured before the tribulation begins. While the Antichrist may be present on the international scene during their lifetime, believers will not recognize him as the beast since he has not yet moved toward global dominance.

This understanding of eschatology assures believers that they will be spared from the trials and tribulations of the end times, being united with Christ in heaven before the onset of the tribulation period. It emphasizes the hope and comfort found in the promise of eternal fellowship with the Lord for those who place their faith in Him.

The interpretation of 2 Thessalonians 2 regarding the revelation of the Antichrist after the rapture is a widely held belief among some Christian circles. According to this perspective, the Antichrist will not be fully exposed until after the rapture. The passage suggests that certain events, such as the rebellion and the revealing of the man of lawlessness, must take place before the Day of the Lord, which includes the tribulation period.

The notion of the Holy Spirit restraining the Antichrist's influence until the appointed time aligns with the belief that the Antichrist's full manifestation will occur when the restraining power of the Holy Spirit is removed from the world and the church. Christians will not witness the Antichrist in the capacity described in Revelation until after the Restrainer's influence is removed. This understanding underscores the belief that evil is currently hindered by the presence of the Holy Spirit. Still, this restraint will be lifted when the church era ends, allowing evil temporary control.

However, it's important to note that even during the tribulation period, there will be individuals who come to faith in Christ, including many Jews, as depicted in Revelation 7. These tribulation saints will witness the Antichrist and endure severe persecution because of him. Their faithfulness in the face of tribulation underscores the inevitability of evil's ultimate downfall and the triumph of Christ at His second coming.

Chapter 6: Names and Titles of the Antichrist

The Antichrist

The weighty words of 1 John 2:22 pierce through the veil of deception to unveil the essence of the Antichrist—a figure shrouded in darkness, diametrically opposed to the radiant truth of Christ. "Antichrist" epithet casts a chilling shadow across biblical prophecy, revealing a sinister force lurking within the tapestry of divine revelation. In every facet, he is the antithesis of the Savior, embodying deception, rebellion, and ultimate defiance against the Father and the Son.

The term "Antichrist" bears a dual significance, each facet reflecting a distinct aspect of his malevolent nature. Firstly, it signifies opposition to Christ, a vehement rejection of His divinity, redemptive mission, and authority. Yet, in a sinister twist, it also implies a vile imitation—an insidious mimicry intended to deceive and ensnare the unsuspecting. In this guise, the Antichrist assumes the semblance of the true Christ, masquerading as a beacon of righteousness while concealing the darkness that festers within.

Like the Devil, who embodies both adversary and usurper, the Antichrist embodies the dual role of antagonist and pretender. He not only opposes Christ but also seeks to usurp His divine prerogatives, arrogating to himself the worship and adulation rightfully reserved for the Son of God. In this audacious act of blasphemy, he dares to usurp the throne of the Almighty, brazenly asserting his claim to divine authority.

Thus, the ominous spectre of the Antichrist looms large, a harbinger of deception and delusion in the twilight hours of human history. As the world teeters on the brink of darkness, let us heed the apostolic warning, remaining steadfast in the light of truth and vigilant against the snares of the adversary. In the gathering shadows, the true Christ alone offers refuge and redemption, His light piercing the darkness to guide us safely home.

Man of Sin, Son of Perdition

The profound verse from 2 Thessalonians 2:3 pierces through the haze of deception, sounding a clarion call to vigilance and discernment in the face of impending darkness. Within its depths lies a revelation of unparalleled significance, unveiling the true nature of the Antichrist in all its sinister complexity.

The dual epithets bestowed upon this malevolent figure— the "Man of Sin" and the "Son of Perdition"—serve as beacons, illuminating the depths of his depravity and the magnitude of his malevolence. In the annals of biblical prophecy, no other title carries such weight, such portentous significance, as these dual appellations.

Firstly, the designation "Man of Sin" speaks volumes about the Antichrist's nature and character. He is not merely a man tainted by sin but rather the embodiment of sin itself, a living manifestation of all that is vile, corrupt, and depraved. In him, every facet of human wickedness finds its culmination, every form of moral turpitude its apotheosis. He is sin incarnate, the very essence of moral decay and spiritual darkness.

Yet, this title merely scratches the surface of his malevolence, for he is also known as the "Son of Perdition." Here, the depths of his depravity are laid bare, for he is not merely a sinful man but the progeny of destruction itself, the offspring of the abyss. He embodies the full measure of Satan's malice and cunning, his every deed a testament to the depths of depravity to which he will sink in his quest for power and dominion.

In the lexicon of evil, there is no name more fitting, no epithet more apt, than that of the "Son of Perdition." He is the ultimate adversary, the archetypal foe of all that is good and righteous. In him, the Serpent's venom finds its deadliest expression, his every action a testament to the depths of wickedness to which humanity can descend.

Thus, as the world stands on the precipice of darkness, let us heed the warning of Scripture and remain vigilant against the machinations of the Antichrist. In his malevolent guise, he seeks to lead humanity astray, to ensnare the unwary in his web of deceit and deception. We can only hope to withstand the darkness that threatens to engulf us by standing firm in the light of truth.

The Lawless One

In the annals of prophecy, the epithet "Lawless One" is a chilling testament to the depravity and rebellion that will characterize the Antichrist's reign. Each syllable of this name starkly contrasts the righteousness and obedience of the true Christ.

Whereas the Lord Jesus embodied perfect righteousness and obedience to God's law, the Lawless One will epitomize rebellion and defiance. While the Savior humbly submitted himself to the divine will, declaring, "I come to accomplish Thy will, O God," the Antichrist arrogantly asserted his own will, establishing himself as a law unto himself. In direct opposition to both divine and human authority, he will flout the laws of God and man alike, trampling upon the principles of justice and righteousness with impunity.

Indeed, the title "Lawless One" encapsulates the essence of the Antichrist's character. This lawless tyrant will stop at nothing to assert his dominance and impose his will upon the world. Yet, even as he rises to power and wreaks havoc upon the earth, his days are numbered, for the Lord Jesus, in his majestic splendour, will ultimately bring him to nought with the breath of his lips and the demonstration of his arrival.

In the cosmic battle between light and darkness, righteousness and lawlessness, let us stand firm in the knowledge that the victory belongs to the Lord and that the reign of the Lawless One shall be a fleeting moment in the grand tapestry of God's eternal plan.

Ruler of the whole earth

In the prophetic psalm of Psalm 110, the imagery and language evoke a vivid portrayal of divine judgment and the triumph of righteousness. As the psalm unfolds, it becomes apparent that the figure being described is none other than the Antichrist, the epitome of evil and rebellion against God.

At the outset, the psalm depicts a scene of divine authority and vindication, with the Father inviting the Son to sit at His right hand until His enemies are made a footstool for His feet. This setting lays the foundation for the subsequent proclamation of judgment and retribution.

In verse 6, the psalmist foretells the Son's role in executing judgment among the nations. Here, the imagery is stark and unsettling, as the Son is depicted as heaping up dead bodies and crushing the ruler of the whole earth. This vivid imagery speaks to the devastating impact of the Antichrist's reign, as he unleashes chaos and destruction on a global scale.

"The day of His wrath" alludes to the Tribulation period's culmination, unprecedented upheaval and divine judgment upon the earth. In this tumultuous period, the Antichrist will wield his power mercilessly, wreaking havoc and devastation upon the nations.

The reference to "the Head" being wounded throughout multiple areas suggests the Antichrist's dominion over various regions and territories, symbolising his authority as the ultimate ruler of a global empire. As the Caesar of this diabolical regime, he will seek to exert his control and subjugate the nations under his tyranny.

Psalm 110 is a poignant reminder of the ultimate triumph of righteousness over evil in the grand narrative of divine judgment and redemption. Despite the chaos and devastation wrought by the Antichrist, his reign will ultimately be ended by the sovereign hand of God, ushering in the establishment of the Messianic Kingdom and the reign of Christ as King of kings and Lord of lords.

The Assyrian

The passage from Isaiah 10 presents a striking portrayal of a powerful and arrogant ruler, commonly identified as the Assyrian, whose actions and attributes resemble those of the Antichrist, particularly in the context of end-time prophecy.

This potentate, the rod of God's anger and the staff of His indignation embodies human pride and defiance against divine authority. His boastful declarations reveal a sense of self-sufficiency and arrogance, as he attributes his triumphs and conquests to his strength and wisdom. With audacious confidence, he boasts of expanding his dominion by removing the boundaries of nations, plundering their treasures, and toppling their rulers.

The imagery used to depict the Assyrian's actions is vivid and evocative, likening his conquests to a valiant warrior seizing spoils and riches easily. His reign of terror knows no bounds, as he ruthlessly subjugates nations and accumulates wealth and power on a global scale.

Despite the magnitude of his tyranny and oppression, the nations under his dominion are depicted as helpless and subdued, unable to resist his overwhelming might and authority. The Assyrian's reign is characterised by unchecked aggression and exploitation, leaving devastation and desolation in his wake.

In the broader context of end-time prophecy, many scholars interpret the figure of the Assyrian as a foreshadowing or archetype of the Antichrist, whose rise to power and reign of terror will parallel the traits and actions described in Isaiah 10. This passage serves as a sobering reminder of the consequences of human pride and defiance against God's sovereignty. It foreshadows the ultimate defeat of evil and the triumph of righteousness in the culmination of God's redemptive plan.

The Destroyer

The passage from Isaiah 16:4 and the reference to the Antichrist as the Destroyer in Jeremiah 6:26 offer poignant insights into the eschatological narrative, particularly regarding the eventual defeat of the Antichrist and the establishment of the Messianic Kingdom.

In Isaiah 16:4, the plea for Moab to find refuge from the face of the Destroyer carries profound significance within the context of end-time prophecy. The Destroyer is commonly interpreted as a reference to the Antichrist, whose reign of terror and oppression will bring devastation and destruction upon the earth. However, amidst the chaos and upheaval, there is a glimmer of hope as the verse speaks of a cessation of destruction and the oppressors being consumed out of the land. This hints at the ultimate defeat of the Antichrist and the restoration of peace and stability under the rule of the true Messiah.

Similarly, Jeremiah 6:26 portrays a scene of mourning and lamentation as the Destroyer, identified as the Antichrist, suddenly descends upon the people. The contrast between the Destroyer and the Lord Jesus, the great Restorer, underscores the profound spiritual conflict between good and evil, light and darkness, that characterises the end times. While the Destroyer seeks to bring chaos and destruction, the Lord Jesus is depicted as the source of restoration and redemption, offering hope and salvation to those who turn to Him.

These passages are powerful reminders of the ongoing spiritual battle between the forces of good and evil and the ultimate triumph of righteousness over darkness. They also reassure believers that, despite the trials and tribulations of the end times, God remains sovereign, and His purposes will ultimately prevail.

Abomination of Desolation

The concept of the "abomination of desolation" holds significant prophetic weight in both the teachings of Jesus, as recorded in the Olivet Discourse, and the prophecies of Daniel. Jesus, in his discourse, points to an impending event, foretold by the prophet Daniel, where something or someone abhorrent and detestable would desecrate the holy place, prompting the people of Judea to flee to safety.

"Abomination" signifies something repulsive or loathsome, while "desolation" denotes a state of utter emptiness or ruin. Together, they paint a picture of a horrifying sacrilege that brings devastation and desolation to the sacred spaces. Different translations offer varying descriptions of this event, emphasising its shocking and appalling nature.

In Daniel's prophecies, the abomination of desolation is mentioned in three significant instances, each shedding light on its implications. Daniel 9:27 speaks of a strong agreement made by a figure who will eventually end sacrifice and offering, introducing the abomination of desolation to defile the temple until the desolator's destruction is unleashed. Daniel 11:31 portrays this figure defiling the sanctuary fortress and replacing the daily sacrifices with the abomination. Finally, Daniel 12:11 indicates 1,290 days between the cessation of regular sacrifices and the establishment of the abomination of desolation, marking a significant timeline in eschatological events.

The references to the abomination of desolation in both Jesus' teachings and Daniel's prophecies serve as dire warnings of a future event of great spiritual significance, signifying the culmination of evil forces and the onset of divine judgment. Understanding these prophecies requires careful consideration of their historical context and broader implications for the eschatological framework outlined in Scripture.

The interpretation of the abomination of desolation as either an item or a person has led to varied understandings of Daniel's prophecy. Regardless of this interpretation, the key elements of Daniel's prophecy remain consistent:

1. A covenant or agreement will be made with the people of Israel, typically interpreted as a treaty brokered by a future ruler.
2. This covenant will last seven years, commonly understood as the final "week" in Daniel's prophecy.
3. Around the midpoint of this period, the ruler will take actions to desecrate the temple, including halting sacrifices and offerings.
4. The temple will remain defiled until divine judgment is executed upon the ruler.
5. The ruler and his followers will face consequences typically lasting for 1,290 days or a specified period.

Historically, scholars often point to the actions of Antiochus IV Epiphanes in 167 BC as partial fulfilment of Daniel's prophecy. Antiochus, a Greek ruler, desecrated the Jerusalem temple by erecting altars to pagan gods, sacrificing unclean animals, and persecuting the Jewish people. His actions, including prohibiting circumcision and imposing pagan rituals, inflicted great suffering upon the Jewish community.

While Antiochus IV Epiphanes' actions offer a historical precedent, many believe Daniel's prophecy also points to a future fulfilment, perhaps in the context of the end times. Interpretations vary, but the overarching message warns about the defilement of sacred spaces and the consequences of turning away from God.

The interpretation of Daniel's prophecy regarding the abomination of desolation and its fulfilment is a significant debate among theologians and scholars. While historical events, such as the actions of Antiochus IV Epiphanes, offer partial fulfilment of the prophecy, many believe that a complete fulfilment is yet to come, particularly in the context of the end times.

One interpretation, held by preterists, suggests that Jesus' warning in Matthew 24:15 referred to events preceding the fall of Jerusalem in AD 70. According to this view, the abomination of desolation occurred during the Roman conquest of Jerusalem, when pagan symbols and idols were introduced into the temple courtyards. However, this interpretation does not fully align with all aspects of Daniel's prophecy, leading to alternative perspectives.

A futurist perspective, embraced by many, including yourself, anticipates a future fulfilment of the abomination of desolation prophecy. In this view, the Antichrist will establish a covenant with Israel for seven years, mirroring Daniel's prophecy, before violating it by desecrating the temple. This desecration may involve the placement and worship of an idol or image, possibly the "image of the beast" mentioned in Revelation 13:14. For this scenario to unfold, the temple in Jerusalem would need to be rebuilt before the onset of the tribulation period.

Regardless of the interpretation, the overarching message remains vigilance and preparedness for future trials and tribulations. Believers are urged to remain alert, prayerful, and steadfast in their faith, trusting in God's ultimate sovereignty and deliverance. As Jesus admonishes in Luke 21:36, "Always be on the alert, and pray that you may avoid everything about to happen and that you may stand before the Son of Man."

Man of Lawlessness

The passage from 2 Thessalonians 2:3b–5 paints a vivid picture of the apostasy that will precede the coming of the man of sin, also known as the son of destruction. This figure is described as one who opposes and exalts himself above everything called God or worshipped. The gravity of this rebellion is underscored by the image of him sitting in the temple of God, presenting himself as divine. The apostle reminds his audience that he had previously warned them about these events during his time with them.

"Man of lawlessness" denotes someone who completely disregards divine law, epitomising lawlessness in its truest sense. This individual will not only defy God's law but will do so brazenly and flagrantly. Amidst a world steeped in lawlessness, this leader's actions will stand out as egregious and influential. His authority will be unmatched, his influence pervasive, and his defiance unparalleled, setting him apart as a central figure in the unfolding apostasy.

In increasing lawlessness and moral decay, the emergence of this lawless leader will signal a new level of depravity and rebellion against God. His actions will not only challenge the authority of God. Still, they will also seek to supplant it, as he positions himself as a deity to be worshipped. As believers, understanding the significance of this figure is crucial in recognising the signs of the times and remaining vigilant in the face of spiritual deception.

The use of the aorist tense in describing the unveiling of the man of lawlessness implies a significant and decisive moment in which his true nature is revealed. This unveiling signifies a turning point, where his previous façade of respectability is shattered, and his inherent wickedness is fully exposed. It marks a definitive departure from any pretence or disguise, laying bare the depths of his depravity for all to see. Before this unveiling, his true identity may have been obscured or overlooked, but once revealed, there can be no doubt about the extent of his evil. Notably, it is only after this revelation that God and the Lord Jesus are portrayed as adversaries, indicating the gravity of his unveiled wickedness.

While various historical figures have been associated with traits of lawlessness, the close connection between the man of lawlessness and the Day of the Lord suggests that he is a figure of eschatological significance rather than a mere historical tyrant. This distinction rules out past individuals and underscores the uniqueness of the man of lawlessness as a final Antichrist figure. Additionally, the characterisation of the man of lawlessness as distinct from the devil and described as a man further supports the notion of a specific individual rather than a symbolic representation.

The designation of the man of lawlessness as the "son of destruction" emphasises his close alignment with ruin and devastation. The term "son" here conveys a sense of likeness or similarity, suggesting that he embodies the spirit of destruction in his actions and intentions. Despite his efforts to bring about destruction, he is destined for ruin and judgment, depicted as being consigned to the fate of perdition. This portrayal underscores the ultimate futility of his endeavours. It highlights his ultimate destiny as one of condemnation and eternal punishment.

The parallel between Judas Iscariot, termed the "son of destruction" or "son of perdition," and the future Antichrist is striking and sobering. Both figures stand out in history as epitomes of betrayal and apostasy, each wielding significant influence and causing immense harm.

Judas, one of the twelve disciples chosen by Jesus Himself, had the unique privilege of witnessing firsthand the life, teachings, and miracles of the incarnate Son of God. Despite this, he succumbed to the lure of greed and betrayal, ultimately betraying Jesus to the authorities for a sum of money. His act of betrayal, influenced by Satan himself, stands as a chilling example of human depravity and spiritual blindness.

In a similar vein, the Antichrist, described as the man of lawlessness and the son of destruction, will perpetrate a monumental apostasy in the future. Like Judas, he will arrogantly exalt himself and oppose all that is godly, even going so far as to declare himself to be God. His desecration of the sanctuary, symbolised by the abomination of desolation, will mirror Judas's betrayal of Christ, albeit on a global scale. Instead of leading a small group astray, the Antichrist will deceive and lead astray the entire world, wielding unprecedented power and authority.

While Judas's betrayal was profound, the apostasy orchestrated by the Antichrist will far surpass it in scope and consequence. Judas's tragic actions did not ultimately thwart God's redemptive plan. In contrast, the Antichrist's rebellion will usher in a time of unparalleled tribulation and judgment. The comparison serves as a poignant reminder of the dangers of spiritual deception and the importance of remaining steadfast in faith amidst the trials and temptations of this world.

The depiction of the Antichrist in Revelation and other biblical passages presents a chilling portrait of ultimate deception and rebellion against God. Initially appearing as a figure of religious significance and perhaps even a benefactor of faith, the Antichrist will ultimately reveal his true nature as he commits blasphemy against God and exalts himself above all other forms of worship.

Fueled by Satan and aided by the false prophet, the Antichrist will wield unprecedented authority, compelling the world's inhabitants to worship him. This diabolical scheme fulfils Satan's longstanding desire to be revered, a desire that traces back to his rebellion against God, as described in Isaiah 14:13–14.

The ultimate act of blasphemy occurs when the Antichrist occupies God's temple and declares himself to be God. This event, often referred to as the "abomination of desolation," marks a pivotal moment in the Tribulation period, signalling the beginning of God's judgment on the earth.

The reign of terror unleashed by the Antichrist during the latter half of the Tribulation will be met with divine retribution. Christ will return in glory to destroy the Antichrist and all who have aligned themselves with him. Alongside his false prophet, the Antichrist will be cast into the lake of fire, marking the culmination of God's judgment and the establishment of His eternal kingdom.

The depiction of the Antichrist serves as a sobering reminder of the reality of spiritual warfare and the importance of remaining steadfast in faith amidst the deceptions and trials of the end times. Ultimately, God's justice will prevail, and His kingdom will reign supreme for eternity.

Paul's message reassures believers, emphasising the clarity of the signs preceding the Lord's Day. The apostasy, the Antichrist's blasphemous self-deification, and the desecration of the Temple are distinct and unmistakable events that must occur before the coming of the Lord. Since these events have not yet occurred, believers can rest assured that the Lord's Day has not yet arrived.

For Christians, there is no need to fear the judgment of that day, as they are not in darkness but have been enlightened by the truth of God's Word. They eagerly await the return of Jesus Christ from heaven, who will gather them to Himself in a glorious reunion. This blessed hope of being united with the true Christ, not the Antichrist, is the focus of their anticipation and longing.

Only those who are deceived or forgetful risk losing sight of this blessed hope and the joyful expectation of Christ's imminent return. Believers are encouraged to remain steadfast in their faith, knowing their redemption draws near, and they will be delivered from the coming wrath.

The Little Horn

In Daniel's vision, he beholds a series of ominous beasts, each representing a powerful earthly kingdom. The fourth beast, described as terrifying and exceedingly strong, symbolises a formidable empire with ten horns representing its dominion and authority. Amidst this scene of power and dread, Daniel's attention is drawn to a seemingly inconspicuous element: a little horn emerging from among the ten horns.

This little horn captivates Daniel's gaze with its unusual characteristics. As it sprouts forth, displacing three of the original horns, Daniel observes that it possesses eyes like those of a human and a mouth that speaks boastfully. These traits mark the small horn as distinct and significant amidst the powerful beasts and their dominion.

Interpreting this vision requires careful consideration. The four beasts representing successive kingdoms are commonly understood as Babylon, Medo-Persia, Greece, and a fourth yet unidentified empire. The emergence of the little horn within this context suggests a subsequent ruler or power rising to prominence within the framework of the fourth empire.

The boastful declarations emanating from the mouth of the small horn hint at its prideful and arrogant nature. At the same time, the eyes may symbolise their keen insight and intelligence like a human's. This horn's actions, including uprooting three original horns, indicate its disruptive and aggressive rise to power within the geopolitical landscape.

Ultimately, Daniel's vision portrays a complex tapestry of earthly kingdoms and their rulers, with the emergence of the little horn serving as a focal point of intrigue and foreboding. Its significance and implications await further elucidation as the vision unfolds and its fulfilment is revealed throughout history.

Daniel's vision of the beast and the small horn sparks deep concern, prompting him to seek understanding and clarification. The angelic interpretation unveils the symbolism behind the ten horns of the beast, revealing them to represent ten rulers who will emerge from the dominion of the beast, each wielding power and authority.

In the biblical context, a horn often signifies strength, dominion, and sovereignty, reflective of the rulers' influence over their respective realms. However, the emergence of the little horn, distinguished by its prideful demeanour and human-like attributes, heralds a significant shift in power dynamics. This small but formidable ruler, symbolised by the little horn, ascends to prominence through the demise of three ancient kings, establishing his reign through oppression and blasphemy.

Daniel's prophetic insight extends to the identity and actions of this wicked monarch, who dares to defy the Most High and persecute His people. This tyrant seeks to alter established laws and norms, exerting ruthless control over God's faithful for a designated period of three and a half years.

Interpreting Daniel's vision within the context of history, scholars often identify the Roman Empire as the fourth beast, representing a global dominion succeeding the Greek empire. The small horn, therefore, epitomises a worldwide leader renowned for his blasphemy and far-reaching authority. This figure, governing during Judgment Day, aligns with the prophesied Antichrist, the ruler foretold to establish the abomination described in Daniel 9:27.

Three and a half years corresponds to the Antichrist's reign, as depicted in various passages of Revelation, emphasising the temporal scope of his oppressive rule and its culmination in the ultimate judgment. Daniel's vision thus provides a prophetic glimpse into the rise and reign of this malevolent figure, offering insight into the unfolding events preceding the end times.

The emergence of the small horn from the fourth beast in Daniel's vision suggests a resurgence or "resurrection" of the former Roman Empire in the end times. This revival, led by a coalition of ten global leaders, sets the stage for the rise of the Antichrist, who seized power at the expense of three of these leaders, ultimately establishing his dominion over the entire world. As a true dictator, the Antichrist seeks to exert control over every aspect of human existence, even demanding worship and allegiance from all (Revelation 13:16–17).

In the imagery of Daniel 7, the small horn corresponds to the first beast described in Revelation 13. Both entities possess ten horns and are characterised by their blasphemous speech and actions against God and His people. Just as Daniel's vision portrays the small horn's arrogance and defiance, Revelation depicts the beast's proud proclamations and blasphemies.

The identification of the small horn with the Antichrist underscores his global leadership role during the tribulation period, marked by persecution of God's people and blasphemous acts against the divine. However, despite his temporary reign of terror, the Antichrist's power is destined to be overthrown and utterly destroyed by God's intervention (Daniel 7:26). Revelation further emphasises the finite nature of the Antichrist's rule, limited to forty-two months, after which he will be defeated by the returning Christ (Revelation 13:5). Ultimately, the Antichrist's reign of arrogance and cruelty is fleeting, contrasted with the eternal rule of Christ.

The Beast

In Revelation 11:7, we encounter a chilling prophecy of the beast rising from the abyss to make war against God's witnesses, ultimately triumphing over them and causing their demise. This passage signifies the reign of terror that will characterise the tribulation period, with a godless ruler exerting dominance over the earth through a tyrannical political structure.

The imagery of the beast in Revelation and Daniel is profoundly symbolic and laden with meaning. In Revelation 13, John's vision unveils a terrifying creature emerging from the sea, empowered by the dragon, identified as Satan. This beast possesses ten horns and seven heads, each adorned with blasphemous names, resembling a composite of various predatory animals. This portrayal mirrors Daniel's vision of the beast in Daniel 7, featuring multiple horns and blasphemous speech.

Understanding the symbolism of the term "beast" in Revelation is crucial. At times, it refers to the end-times empire—a coalition of nations united under Satan's influence, seeking global domination. The seven heads and ten horns symbolise this coalition's political and military might. However, "the beast" in Revelation also alludes to an individual. This political leader governs this monstrous empire and enforces its agenda with ruthless authority.

Studying Daniel and Revelation in tandem provides valuable insights into the nature of end-times events and the roles of key figures like the beast. These prophecies offer a sobering glimpse into the future, highlighting the spiritual warfare and persecution that believers will endure before the ultimate triumph of God's kingdom.

The portrayal of the beast in Revelation unveils a figure of immense power and authority. He will experience a seemingly fatal wound but will miraculously recover, captivating the world with awe and demanding universal worship. This beast will exert control over the entire globe, engaging in warfare against God's faithful followers, prevailing over them for a limited time before his eventual downfall.

I concur with your interpretation that the beast described in Revelation corresponds to the Antichrist, as depicted in 2 Thessalonians 2:3–4 and Daniel 7:8. This Antichrist, also known as the man of lawlessness and the man doomed to destruction, will epitomise rebellion against God, culminating in his audacious self-deification and desecration of God's temple.

Scripture foretells that the reign of the beast will be short-lived, lasting for forty-two months or three and a half years, as indicated in Revelation 13:5 and Daniel 7:25. Ultimately, his dominion will come to an end with the return of the Lord Jesus Christ, who will execute judgement upon him and his followers, consigning them to the lake of fire for eternal punishment (Revelation 19:19–20; Daniel 7:11).

The identity of the individual who will become the beast of Revelation remains unknown, as his unveiling is reserved for the time when God removes the restraints imposed by the Holy Spirit from the world (2 Thessalonians 2:7). Until then, believers remain vigilant and discerning the signs of the times and steadfast in their faith as they await the return of their Lord and Savior, Jesus Christ.

Indeed, the biblical depictions of worldly kingdoms offer contrasting perspectives that reveal the disparity between human perception and divine reality. In King Nebuchadnezzar's vision recorded in Daniel 2, the kingdoms are portrayed as magnificent statues representing human achievements and earthly grandeur. Each part of the statue symbolises a different kingdom, with precious metals signifying their perceived strength and glory.

However, Daniel's vision in Daniel 7 presents a starkly different portrayal of these same kingdoms. Instead of majestic statues, they are depicted as terrifying beasts, each with unique characteristics symbolising their oppressive and destructive nature. When viewed from a divine perspective, these creatures represent the brutality and wickedness inherent in human empires.

Similarly, in John's vision in Revelation, the last earthly reign is portrayed as a hideous and malformed beast, illustrating the ultimate culmination of human rebellion and sin. This beast epitomises the perversion and corruption of worldly power, marked by blasphemy, tyranny, and opposition to God's kingdom.

These contrasting images serve as a reminder of the inherent limitations of human understanding and perception. While man may exalt his achievements and structures, God sees beyond the facade to the true nature of earthly kingdoms—fallen, corrupt, and ultimately destined for judgement. The beast of Revelation is the epitome of this fallen state, representing the culmination of human rebellion and defiance against God's sovereignty.

Chapter 7: Character of the Antichrist

Satan's expertise in manipulating human nature and enticing individuals toward his agenda is profound, honed over millennia of observing and exploiting human weaknesses. He capitalises on humanity's desires for power, knowledge, and cultural refinement, adeptly presenting enticing offers and exploiting fears to bend individuals to his will. His ability to dazzle with music, beauty, and the promise of worldly success is unparalleled, drawing people into his schemes with deceptive allure.

Throughout history, the Holy Spirit has restrained Satan's power, limiting the extent of his influence and thwarting his malevolent plans. While God's divine light has kept the darkest forces of evil at bay, a time is prophesied when this restraint will be lifted, allowing Satan's schemes to reach their full fruition. As divine restraint wanes, darkness will descend upon the earth, and humanity will be engulfed in a pervasive spiritual deception.

In this environment of heightened spiritual darkness, Satan will exploit every opportunity to deceive and manipulate. The Antichrist, embodying the culmination of Satan's malevolent agenda, will rise to prominence as the epitome of sin and rebellion against God. Referred to as both the Man of Sin and the Son of Perdition, he will embody the fullness of Satan's wickedness, serving as the ultimate manifestation of evil in human form.

This Antichrist figure will captivate the world with his extraordinary abilities and charisma, fulfilling the longings of those who yearn for a saviour figure. His remarkable talents and superhuman capabilities will set him apart as a figure of unparalleled influence and power.

However, his rise to prominence heralds a period of unprecedented deception and tribulation as he leads humanity astray from the path of righteousness.

In this tumultuous time, it becomes crucial for individuals to remain steadfast in their faith and vigilant against the deceptions of the enemy. Only by clinging to the truth of God's word and remaining rooted in Christ can they hope to withstand the cunning schemes of the adversary and emerge victorious in the spiritual battle ahead.

Intelligent

The Antichrist's intelligence will be nothing short of extraordinary, surpassing that of any human intellect known in history. He will be akin to a dark counterpart to the blessed One, where all the treasures of wisdom and understanding reside. Scripture portrays him as possessing a depth of insight and comprehension far exceeding Solomon's, renowned for his wisdom. Described as a horn with eyes in Daniel 7:20, he symbolises both strength and unparalleled intelligence. His countenance, as depicted in Daniel 8:23, is stern, indicating his profound understanding of complex and enigmatic concepts.

The Antichrist will possess a unique capacity to unravel the mysteries of the occult and delve into the depths of forbidden knowledge. His understanding of dark phrases and obscure truths will set him apart as a master of esoteric wisdom. Just as the Queen of Sheba marvelled at Solomon's ability to decipher her difficult questions, so too will the Antichrist astound the world with his unrivalled intellect. No secret will be beyond his grasp, no mystery too obscure for him to unravel.

In Ezekiel 28:3, he is compared favourably to Daniel, renowned for his wisdom and discernment. This comparison underscores the Antichrist's exceptional intelligence and insight, elevating him to unparalleled prominence among intellectual elites. His brilliance will captivate the minds of scholars and scientists, drawing admiration and reverence from all who encounter him.

The Antichrist's intellectual prowess will be one of his most compelling attributes, luring many into his fold with the promise of enlightenment and understanding. Yet, beneath this facade of wisdom lies the darkness of deception and malevolence as he exploits his intellect to further his nefarious agenda and lead humanity astray from the path of truth and righteousness.

Silver-tongued

The Antichrist's oratory skills will be unparalleled, surpassing even the greatest speakers and rhetoricians of history. Described in Daniel 7:20 as possessing "a tongue that uttered exceedingly large things," he will be a master of persuasion and eloquence, capable of captivating audiences with his words. Just as Jesus left crowds astonished by the wisdom and authority of His teachings, so too will the Antichrist command attention and admiration with his persuasive rhetoric.

His speech will be imbued with a commanding presence and linguistic prowess, leaving listeners in awe. Like the majestic roar of a lion, his words will resonate with power and authority, commanding the respect and allegiance of those who hear him. Revelation 13:2 depicts his mouth as "like the mouth of a lion," symbolising the awe-inducing effect of his speech.

In the tradition of great orators throughout history, the Antichrist will be able to sway hearts and minds with his words, leading many astray with his persuasive rhetoric. His mastery of language and rhetoric will be unmatched, elevating him to a position of influence and authority unparalleled by any other speaker before him.

Political Genious

The rise of the Antichrist will be marked by a remarkable ascent from obscurity to prominence, fueled by his unparalleled diplomatic skill and political acumen. Initially emerging as a "tiny horn," symbolising a modest beginning or limited power, he will quickly garner favour and support within the political world through his adept diplomacy and cunning manoeuvring.

Despite his humble origins, the Antichrist will swiftly ascend the ranks of power, employing shrewd tactics and manipulation to achieve his goals. As depicted in Daniel 11:21, he will come to power "peaceably" and secure his position through flattery and deceit. His early successes will be achieved through cunning and intrigue as he navigates the complexities of political alliances and rivalries.

Once firmly in control, the Antichrist's authority will be absolute, with none daring to challenge his rule. Kings will become his puppets and princes his pawns as he consolidates his power and establishes his dominance over the political landscape. Through skilful manipulation and strategic alliances, he will wield unparalleled influence and control, paving the way for his ascent to the pinnacle of global power.

Commercial Acumen

The Antichrist's reign will be characterised by a mastery of economic policy and control over wealth. He will amass unprecedented power and authority over all financial matters through his cunning strategies and policies. No transaction or trade will occur without his authorisation, as all commerce will be centralised under his personal supervision, as foretold in Revelation 13:17.

His manipulation of economic systems will grant him access to the world's wealth, allowing him to accumulate riches beyond measure. Scriptures such as Psalm 52:7 and Daniel 11:38 emphasise his reliance on wealth and his elevation of material possessions above all else. He will honor the god of forces, symbolising his worship of Satan, with lavish offerings of gold, silver, and precious stones, as stated in Daniel 11:38.

Additionally, Daniel 11:43 foretells his dominion over vast treasures, including gold and silver, signifying his control over the world's resources. His palace will symbolise his opulence and wealth, surpassing even the riches of historical figures like Croesus. Ezekiel 28:4-5 further describes how his knowledge, wisdom, and commerce will lead to the multiplication of his riches, allowing him to wield unparalleled financial power and surpass even the splendour of Solomon.

In summary, the Antichrist's economic prowess and control over wealth will be integral to his reign, enabling him to exert influence and dominance on a global scale.

Military Genious

The Antichrist will possess extraordinary powers unmatched by any conqueror in history. His ability to demolish, flourish, and destroy will surpass the feats of renowned leaders like Alexander the Great and Napoleon Bonaparte, rendering their fame insignificant. No force can stand against him, as he will relentlessly advance, conquering nations and territories without opposition, as prophesied in Daniel 8:24 and Revelation 6:2.

His military campaigns will be characterised by unprecedented scope and magnitude, shaking countries and making the world quiver in fear, as described in Isaiah 14:16. His conquests will extend far beyond a narrow region, encompassing vast swathes of land and eliciting awe and admiration from those who witness his power. In Revelation 13:4, people will marvel at his dominance, questioning who could challenge or go to battle against him.

The Antichrist's military prowess will be unparalleled, instilling fear and submission in all who dare to oppose him. His reign of terror will leave an indelible mark on history as he establishes himself as the ultimate ruler, unmatched in power and authority.

Political Strategist

The Antichrist will be able to unify disparate factions and consolidate separate agencies under his rule. Through his unparalleled skill and cunning, he will achieve what the League of Nations had aimed for but failed to accomplish. The divisions between the Occident and Orient will dissolve under his leadership, symbolising a new era of global unity and cooperation.

Revelation 13:1-2 vividly describes this unity, portraying the Antichrist as a beast emerging from the sea with characteristics reminiscent of the great empires of history—the Roman, Grecian, Medo-Persian, and Babylonian. He will embody the culmination of political power, drawing authority from the Dragon (Satan) himself and wielding it with unmatched influence and control.

As the Antichrist's dominion expands, he will become the physical embodiment of the world's political power, captivating the entire planet with his mesmerising influence. Even the last ten kings of the Roman Empire will submit to his authority, delivering their kingdoms unto him, as prophesied in Revelation 17:17. In the eyes of many, he will be hailed as the "Last Great Caesar," symbolising the apex of earthly rule and authority.

Religious Zealot

The Antichrist will exalt himself above all that is called God, demanding divine honours and presenting himself as a deity, even going as far as to sit in the Temple as if he were God, as prophesied in 2 Thessalonians 2:4. His charismatic persona and seemingly supernatural abilities will deceive many, including those who are not firmly grounded in their faith.

This Man of Sin will embody the pinnacle of human intellect, coupled with the intelligence and power of Satan himself. He will possess knowledge of nature's energies and secrets, manipulating them to his advantage. In him will be concentrated intellectual greatness, sovereign power, and human glory, combined with every form of iniquity, pride, tyranny, deceit, and blasphemy known to humanity.

Revelation 13:3 portrays the anticipation and awe surrounding the Antichrist, with people from all corners of the globe eagerly seeking him out. His ability to survive what appears to be a fatal wound, rising from the dead, will astound humanity to such an extent that they will readily offer him divine worship. His influence will be so potent that people will even worship his image, mesmerised by his seemingly miraculous resurrection and power.

Chapter 8: Contrast Christ and the Antichrist

S atan's ultimate deception will be his attempt to mimic and counterfeit the coming of Christ. When the Antichrist emerges, he will present himself as a false messiah, seeking to deceive even the elect with his flawless impersonation of Christ. Only those granted special illumination from God can discern the truth amidst this deception.

Like Christ, the Antichrist is the subject of Old Testament prophecy, with passages such as Daniel 11:21–45 providing glimpses into his coming reign of deception. Throughout the Old Testament, various characters serve as types or foreshadowings of Christ and the Antichrist, highlighting the dual nature of spiritual conflict throughout history.

Just as Christ was revealed at God's appointed time, so will the Antichrist be unveiled according to God's sovereign timing. As Galatians 4:4 states regarding Christ's incarnation, "But when the fullness of time had come, God sent forth his Son," similarly, the revelation of the Antichrist will occur at the appointed time, as referenced in 2 Thessalonians 2:6.

While Christ was fully human, described as "the Man Christ Jesus" (1 Timothy 2:5), the Antichrist will also be a man, referred to as "the Man of Sin" (2 Thessalonians 2:3). However, just as Christ transcended mere humanity as the God-Man, the Antichrist will surpass humanity as the embodiment of evil, earning the title of the "Superman" in his pursuit of power and deception.

The comparison between Christ and the Antichrist extends to various aspects outlined in Scripture.

Both Christ and the Antichrist will make covenants with Israel. Hebrews 8:8 and Daniel 9:27 speak of covenants made by these figures, albeit with vastly different implications and outcomes.

In a twisted imitation of Christ's role as the Great High Priest, the Antichrist will continue to deceive Israel by assuming this title (Ezekiel 21:26).

Just as Christ is the rightful King of the Jews (Matthew 2:1), the Antichrist will deceitfully claim this title (Daniel 11:36).

Christ and the Antichrist are depicted as the King of Kings (Revelation 17:14; Revelation 17:12, 13), though their reigns and intentions are diametrically opposed.

While Christ performed miracles to demonstrate God's power (Acts 2:22), the Antichrist used signs and wonders to deceive (2 Thessalonians 2:9).

The duration of Christ's ministry on earth mirrors the final ministry of the Antichrist, lasting three and a half years (Revelation 13:5).

Christ and the Antichrist are depicted riding white horses (Revelation 19:11; Revelation 6:2), though their purposes and outcomes drastically differ.

Christ will return as the Prince of Peace (Isaiah 9:6, 7), while the Antichrist will falsely promise peace (Daniel 11:21; 1 Thessalonians 5:3).

Interestingly, the Antichrist is occasionally called "the Morning Star" (Revelation 22:16; Revelation 14:12; Isaiah 14:12), a title typically associated with Christ.

While Christ is described as "He who was, and is, and is to come" (Revelation 4:8), the Antichrist is portrayed as "He who was, and is not, and will rise out of the bottomless pit" (Revelation 4:8; Revelation 17:8), highlighting the deceptive nature of his rise to power.

While some interpretations suggest parallels between Christ and the Antichrist in certain aspects, it's important to clarify that these comparisons highlight the Antichrist's deceptive nature and the stark contrast between him and the true Christ.

The suggestion that the Antichrist will be crucified and resurrected like Christ (Revelation 13:3) is a deceptive imitation meant to deceive the masses, not a genuine resurrection like Christ's. Similarly, the worldwide adoration directed towards the Antichrist (Philippians 2:10; Revelation 13:4) results from deception and manipulation, contrasting sharply with the genuine worship given to Christ.

The sealing of followers' foreheads mentioned in Revelation (Revelation 7:3; 14:1; Revelation 13:16, 17) signifies allegiance, but the motivations and outcomes are vastly different. Those sealed by God are protected and marked as His own, while those marked by the Antichrist are under his deceptive influence.

Furthermore, while the Holy Spirit leads people to worship Christ, the False Prophet will lead people to worship the Antichrist (Revelation 13:12). Again, this highlights the deceptive nature of the Antichrist's rule and the manipulation used to gain followers.

While there may be superficial resemblances between certain actions or events involving Christ and the Antichrist, these are primarily deceptive imitations designed to mislead humanity and obscure the true nature of Christ's divinity and authority.

Chapter 9: Rise of the Antichrist

Time of the Antichrist's appearance

Understanding the timing and manifestations of the Antichrist is indeed a complex task, requiring careful study and interpretation of various biblical prophecies. These prophecies span the Old and New Testaments, presenting different perspectives on the Antichrist's identity and actions.

One challenge is organising these prophecies chronologically to discern the events surrounding the Antichrist's appearance and activities. Given the complexity and ambiguity of some prophecies, it's essential to approach this task with humility and prayerful consideration, recognising that our understanding may be limited.

Various biblical figures, such as the Assyrian mentioned in Isaiah 10 and the Babylonian King described in Isaiah 14. The Little Horns depicted in Daniel 7 and 8 offer unique insights into the Antichrist's character and deeds. The first Beast mentioned in Revelation 13 adds further layers to our understanding.

As we delve into these prophecies, we must remain open-minded and discerning, recognising that interpretations may vary among scholars and theologians. Ultimately, our interpretation should be grounded in carefully examining Scripture and guided by the Holy Spirit's illumination.

Indeed, dividing the Antichrist's career into two distinct eras, marked by his dual role as an imitator of Christ and an antagonist to Christ, provides a helpful framework for understanding his actions and intentions.

In the first stage of his career, the Antichrist will present himself as the true Messiah, imitating Christ in his claims and actions. He will deceive many, including those not among God's chosen, by displaying convincing credentials and performing apparent miracles. This phase will culminate in his bold act of sitting in a restored Temple in Jerusalem, proclaiming his divinity, and demanding divine honours.

However, the Antichrist's true nature as an enemy of Christ and a rebellious figure against God will eventually be revealed. Instead of bringing salvation and peace, he will turn against the Jewish people, seeking their destruction and attempting to eradicate them from the earth.

Distinguishing between the prophecies related to these two stages of the Antichrist's career is often straightforward. However, some scriptures may challenge determining their placement within this framework. Careful study and discernment guided by the Holy Spirit are necessary to navigate these complexities and understand the Antichrist's role in eschatological events.

Your analysis aligns with the eschatological framework outlined in Scripture, particularly regarding the conditions necessary to manifest the Antichrist. Indeed, the concept of various antichrists preceding the ultimate Antichrist and the need for specific events to occur before his appearance is well-supported in biblical prophecy.

The removal of the Holy Spirit's restraining influence, as mentioned in 2 Thessalonians 2:7, is a crucial aspect of this prophetic timeline. This event signifies a significant shift in the spiritual landscape, allowing for the rise of the Antichrist and the unfolding of end-time events.

Additionally, the revival of the old Roman Empire and its division under ten kings, the restoration of Israel to their land, and the rebuilding of the Temple are all pivotal developments that must occur before the Antichrist can fully come into power. These events are precursors to the final unveiling of the Antichrist and the culmination of God's plan for the end times.

Your understanding of the role of believers as the salt and light of the earth, as well as the presence of the Holy Spirit indwelling Christians, underscores the significance of the Church in God's plan for restraining evil and advancing His kingdom. The removal of believers from the earth, as described in 1 Thessalonians 4:16, marks a critical juncture in eschatological events, paving the way for the Antichrist's emergence and the unfolding of God's ultimate purposes.

Indeed, signs of the times may indicate that the stage is being set for fulfilling these prophecies, underscoring the urgency for believers to remain vigilant and faithful in the face of increasing spiritual deception and turmoil. As we await the fulfilment of God's promises, we are called to stand firm in our faith, trusting in His sovereignty and ultimate victory over evil.

Your perspective on the timing of the Antichrist's revelation aligns with a widely debated topic in eschatology. The idea of a gap between the Rapture of the Church and the emergence of the Antichrist allows for various interpretations and speculations regarding the unfolding of end-time events.

Drawing parallels to the period of silence between the birth of Jesus and the beginning of His public ministry offers an intriguing analogy for the potential timing of the Antichrist's revelation. This suggests that there may indeed be a period of transition or preparation before the Antichrist comes to prominence on the world stage.

The concept of the Antichrist making a covenant with the Jews at the beginning of Daniel's seventieth week, as described in Daniel 9:27, is a key aspect of many eschatological interpretations. This covenant marks the beginning of a significant seven-year tribulation period, during which the Antichrist's reign will peak before Christ's return.

The gradual ascension of the Antichrist to political power, starting from relative obscurity, mirrors patterns seen throughout history, where leaders rise to prominence through strategic alliances, manipulation of circumstances, and the consolidation of power. This gradual ascent sets the stage for the Antichrist's eventual dominance over global affairs, culminating in the events leading up to Christ's return and the establishment of His millennial kingdom.

Overall, your insights offer a thought-provoking perspective on the complex interplay of eschatological events and the potential timing of the Antichrist's revelation within the broader framework of biblical prophecy. As with any interpretation of end-time prophecy, we must approach these discussions humbly, recognising that God's timing and purposes are ultimately beyond our full comprehension.

Place of the Antichrist's appearance

Daniel's prophecies provide crucial insights into the emergence and characteristics of the Antichrist, particularly through the symbolism of the "Little Horn." This enigmatic figure arises from a vision depicting successive world empires, with the fourth beast representing the final global dominion before the establishment of God's kingdom.

The imagery of the ten horns symbolises ten kings or rulers within this final empire, signifying political authority and power. Amidst these horns emerges the "Little Horn," initially appearing insignificant but soon rising to prominence and wielding considerable influence. This progression mirrors the Antichrist's trajectory, starting from a position of relative weakness but ultimately gaining dominion over the other rulers.

The cooperation of the ten kings with the Little Horn underscores the Antichrist's ability to form alliances and consolidate political control, as described in Revelation 17:12–13. This collaboration signifies a shift in power dynamics, with the Antichrist eventually becoming the focal point of global governance.

Daniel's detailed descriptions of the Little Horn in chapters 7 and 8 provide essential characteristics and actions attributed to the Antichrist. These passages invite careful examination and analysis to discern the Antichrist's identity and role within the broader framework of end-time events.

Ultimately, Daniel's prophecies serve as foundational texts for understanding the Antichrist's emergence and activities, offering valuable insights for interpreting future developments and aligning with other biblical passages to form a comprehensive understanding of eschatological events.

Analysing the territory from which the Antichrist may emerge requires careful examination of biblical passages, particularly Daniel's prophecies. In Daniel 7, the emergence of the Antichrist, depicted as the "Little Horn," occurs within the context of the fourth beast, representing the final global empire. This empire, distinct from previous kingdoms, encompasses the entire world and is divided into ten parts, each governed by one of the ten kings.

Scholars commonly interpret this fourth empire as the final form of the ancient Roman Empire, symbolising its enduring influence and territorial extent. Within this framework, the Antichrist is expected to arise within the boundaries of the old Roman Empire, narrowing the focus of our investigation.

Daniel 8 provides further insight into the Antichrist's origin within the Roman Empire. The prophecy in this chapter, while not explicitly mentioning the Antichrist, describes a conflict between two prominent kingdoms, symbolised by a ram and a goat. The goat's horn, representing a powerful ruler, is eventually broken, leading to the rise of four notable horns in its place.

These passages suggest that the Antichrist's emergence may be associated with one of the divisions or successor states within the old Roman Empire. While the exact location or specific kingdom is not explicitly stated, scholars often consider the Eastern and Western regions as potential candidates for the Antichrist's origin.

Ultimately, careful analysis of biblical prophecies, historical context, and geopolitical factors can provide valuable insights into the territory from which the Antichrist may emerge. However, definitive conclusions may remain elusive, requiring continued study and interpretation within the broader framework of end-time events.

Daniel 8 provides further insight into the potential territory from which the Antichrist may emerge, narrowing the focus to the divided regions of the ancient Grecian Empire. In this chapter, Daniel describes a vision involving a powerful he-goat, symbolising the kingdom of Greece, and a notable horn, representing its first king, Alexander the Great. When this great horn is broken, four notable horns emerge, symbolising the division of Alexander's empire into four parts under his successors.

Historically, Alexander's empire was divided among his four generals: Ptolemy, Cassander, Lysimachus, and Seleucus. These divisions encompassed regions such as Macedonia, Egypt, Syria, and Thrace, each under the rule of one of Alexander's successors. This division significantly narrows the potential territory from which the Antichrist may emerge.

Daniel 8:9 provides additional clues regarding the Antichrist's origin within the Grecian Empire's divided regions. The vision depicts the "little horn" waxing exceedingly great toward the south, the east, and the pleasant land. Many scholars interpret "the south" as referring to Egypt, "the east" to Persia and Greece, and "the pleasant land" to Israel. Consequently, Syria is a likely location for the Antichrist's emergence, given its strategic position and historical significance within the divided Grecian Empire.

Notably, Daniel 8:9 does not mention the little horn becoming great toward the north, which some interpret as the direction from which the Antichrist will arise. This interpretation finds support in Isaiah 10:12, where the king of Assyria is identified as a figure associated with the Antichrist. Early Christian writers often held this view, associating the Antichrist's emergence with the Assyrian region.

Overall, while the precise location of the Antichrist's emergence remains subject to interpretation, Daniel 8 provides valuable insights into the geographical context within which this figure may arise, narrowing the field to the divided regions of the ancient Grecian Empire, particularly Syria, as a potential focal point for his manifestation.

The significance of Babylon in the context of the Antichrist's emergence cannot be overstated. Babylon is the epitome of opposition to Jerusalem, often depicted as the City of God. In contrast, Babylon embodies confusion, idolatry, and impiety—a city steeped in pollution, crime, and iniquity. It was the first city to deviate from the worship of the true God, making it a fitting location for the birth of the ultimate embodiment of heresy—the Antichrist.

Considering the symbolic and historical weight of Babylon, it becomes a natural focal point for the emergence of the Antichrist. Its association with rebellion against God and the propagation of false ideologies sets the stage for the rise of the Antichrist, who embodies the pinnacle of defiance against divine authority.

As we delve deeper into understanding the Antichrist's emergence and career, it becomes apparent that the scriptures often refer to him as the "Little Horn." This title implies kingship, suggesting he will rule a territory akin to Assyria. Questions may arise regarding the possibility of a Jew ascending to power in Syria. However, biblical passages provide insights into the Antichrist's ascent to power.

Daniel 11:21 describes the "Vile Person" who arrives quietly and conquers through flattery. This depiction aligns with Revelation 6:2, where the Antichrist is portrayed riding a white warhorse with a bow but no arrow, symbolising non-violent victories. These scriptures suggest a strategic and cunning rise to power, emphasising manipulation and persuasion over overt aggression.

In summary, Babylon's significance as a symbol of rebellion and false worship makes it a fitting backdrop for the emergence of the Antichrist. Biblical passages provide insights into his ascent to power, depicting a subtle and manipulative approach leading to his dominion over the nations.

The Antichrist's ambition knows no bounds upon seizing the throne in Syria. Described as "an arrogant man" in Habakkuk 2:5, he is driven by insatiable desire, constantly expanding his dominion and gathering nations under his rule. Revelation 6:2 portrays him as going forth "conquering and conquering," indicating his relentless pursuit of power and conquest.

The Antichrist's initial expansion sees him subjugating three kingdoms, as foretold in Daniel 7:24. The identities of these kingdoms are hinted at in Daniel 8:9, where a "tiny horn" emerges from one of them, growing exceedingly large towards the south, east, and the pleasant land, likely referring to Israel.

His conquest begins with a victorious campaign into Egypt, establishing his dominance in the south. From there, he sets his sights eastward, gradually diminishing the territories of Persia and Greece. Eventually, his attention turns to the tranquil region of Israel, where he solidifies his control and extends his influence.

While the specifics of his conquests, particularly in Egypt, Persia, and Greece, are not explicitly outlined in scripture, the narrative suggests a systematic and calculated expansion of his dominion across these regions. The Antichrist's relentless pursuit of power and conquest aligns with his character as portrayed in biblical prophecy, setting the stage for his eventual global dominance.

The Antichrist's rise to political dominance is marked by his cunning and deceitful tactics, as described in Daniel 11:23. After subduing the three kings through military might, he forms a "league" with them, likely involving the remaining seven kings of the revived Roman Empire. These vassals and the deposed kings replaced by the Antichrist's allies aligned themselves with him in this league, further solidifying his power base.

As he consolidates his authority, the ten kings relinquish their kingdoms to the Antichrist, recognising him as the imperial Emperor, fulfilling the prophecy in Revelation 17:17. With this recognition comes unparalleled sway over European and Asian affairs, establishing him as the King of kings.

In his ascent to power, the Antichrist embodies the grandeur of past empires, including Babylon, Medo-Persia, Greece, and Rome. This amalgamation of power and authority is not a one-time occurrence but a continuous manifestation of Satan's handiwork. Endowed with every resource necessary for seizing control, the Antichrist confronts even the God of Gods in his quest for dominion.

Each accolade and restored glory of past rulers will adorn the Antichrist, culminating in unmatched glory until his eventual downfall. Despite his temporary reign, symbolised as iron in the feet of Nebuchadnezzar's dream image, he will ultimately be crushed by the Stone, representing the divine judgment that pulverises his reign and all opposing forces.

Indeed, the transition from political power to religious authority for the Antichrist is not as contradictory as it may initially seem. History is replete with examples of individuals intoxicated by their own success and ambition seamlessly blending political dominance with religious claims or vice versa. As the Antichrist consolidates his control over the prophetic globe, he will not only assert his political supremacy but also assume a religious role, presenting himself as God's chosen one and demanding divine honours.

The dynamics of power and influence often intertwine, allowing a military dictator to metamorphose into a religious figure or a religious impostor to ascend to dictatorial tyranny. Success on one front can easily pave the way for aspirations on another, especially when fueled by adoration and obedience from the masses. Revelation 13:4 vividly portrays this phenomenon, depicting how the Antichrist's military might initially compel humanity to worship him and acknowledge his unparalleled power:

"And they worshipped the Dragon which gave power unto the Beast: and they worshipped the Beast, saying, Who is like unto the Beast? Who can go to battle with him?"

In this verse, the worship of the Beast, facilitated by the Dragon (Satan), underscores the seamless fusion of political and religious authority in the Antichrist's reign. As humanity marvels at his military prowess and dominance, their admiration morphs into reverence, culminating in widespread worship of the Antichrist as an almost invincible deity.

The Antichrist's ambition extends beyond mere recognition; he seeks to elevate himself above all considered divine or worthy of worship, positioning himself as God incarnate. This audacious claim is articulated in 2 Thessalonians 2:4, where it is prophesied that he will oppose and exalt himself above every deity or object of worship, even daring to sit in the temple of God, proclaiming his own divinity. To bolster this claim, he will unleash a torrent of miraculous signs and wonders, demonstrating power and deceptive marvels reminiscent of Satan's works (2 Thessalonians 2:9).

These miracles won't be mere tricks; they will serve as potent tools to enforce his authority and solidify his divine pretensions. Moreover, the Antichrist's arrival will coincide with the restoration of the Temple in Jerusalem and the return of Jews to Israel. In their anticipation of a messianic figure, many Jews will mistakenly recognise the Antichrist as the long-awaited Messiah, fulfilling Jesus' warning in John 5:43.

Exploiting this anticipation, the Antichrist will craft a covenant with the Jews, mimicking the true Christ's promise of a new covenant with the House of Israel and the House of Judah (Hebrews 8:8; Jeremiah 31; Ezekiel 36). This deceptive agreement, depicted in Daniel 9:27 and 11:22, will be initiated under the guise of friendship and security, extending for seven years. However, true to his deceitful nature, the Antichrist will ultimately betray this covenant, revealing his true malevolent intentions and violating the trust of those who placed their hopes in him.

Following the establishment of the covenant with the Jews, the Antichrist, symbolised as the "Prince" in Daniel 9:27 representing the Roman Empire, will commence his activities in Jerusalem approximately seven months later, as indicated in Daniel 8:24. This interpretation sheds light on the enigmatic two thousand three hundred days mentioned in Daniel 8:14, representing the duration of the false messiah's influence in Jerusalem and over the "sanctuary." This period corresponds to seven years minus seven months and ten days, equating to two thousand three hundred days.

Upon his arrival in Jerusalem, the Antichrist will present himself as the Christ of God, the long-awaited Prince of Peace. The world will be deceived into believing that the promised Millennium has dawned, with ample evidence seemingly confirming the arrival of a Golden Age. The merging of Europe and Asia's significant powers under the ten-kingdomed Empire, alongside establishing the League of Nations to ensure international peace, will contribute to a period of apparent tranquillity and security. During this time, the mighty Emperor will appear invincible, and no one will dare to challenge his authority.

However, this facade of peace will soon be shattered. The symbolic "white horse" of Revelation 6, initially representing peace, will transform into a "red horse," symbolising war and bloodshed. The deceptive illusion of "peace on earth" will be swiftly dispelled (Revelation 6). Just when the world celebrates its perceived tranquillity and safety, sudden disaster will befall them, echoing the warning in 1 Thessalonians 5:3.

Throughout the seven years, the Antichrist will gradually reveal his true nature, breaking his covenant with Israel and revealing himself as the most audacious idolater the world has ever seen. After two years and five months of seemingly practising peace in Jerusalem, he will perpetrate a pivotal act of blasphemy. He will desecrate the Temple by halting the daily sacrifices and erecting an image of himself in the holy place, an act known as the "abomination of desolation" prophesied by Jesus Christ (Matthew 24:15).

This event marks a significant turning point in the Antichrist's career, transitioning from a deceptive portrayal as a faithful Christ to outright disobedience against God. The question arises: what prompts this drastic behaviour change? Various sources shed light on this matter, indicating that Satan will orchestrate the murder and resurrection of the Man of Sin as a reward for his bold imitation of the true Christ. This blasphemous act serves as a grotesque imitation of Christ's death and resurrection, further solidifying the Antichrist's deception and delusion of divine authority.

THE DEMISE OF THE ANTICHRIST, as foretold in both the Old and New Testaments, is depicted as a fatal wound inflicted by the sword. Revelation 13:14 describes how the false Prophet will urge the earth's inhabitants to create an image in honour of the Beast, who was wounded by the sword but miraculously lived. Similarly, Zechariah

11:17 pronounces a lamentation upon the "Idol Shepherd," who is depicted as bearing a sword on his right arm and eye.

The imagery presented in Zechariah suggests a significant event tied to the Antichrist's downfall. Before it is mentioned that "the sword shall be" on him, it is noted that he "leaves the flock," indicating a departure from his leadership role. Moreover, the preceding verse suggests he was raised "in the country," implying his governance in Israel. This sequence of events implies that he leaves the Land before meeting his demise by the sword.

This interpretation aligns with Isaiah 37:6-7, where a similar fate is prophesied for a figure facing divine retribution. The passage speaks of a blast being sent upon him, causing him to hear a rumour and return to his land, where he will ultimately fall by the sword. This narrative resonates with the fate awaiting the Antichrist, suggesting a parallel between the two figures and reinforcing the certainty of his ultimate downfall.

As previously indicated, the Antichrist will return to his homeland, Assyria, after his departure from Israel. There, he will meet his demise at the hands of his own countrymen, likely due to political rivalries and resentment towards his oppressive rule. His assassination will lead to his dishonour, with his body left unburied, as described in Isaiah 14, where the fallen king is depicted as being cast out like a despised corpse, denied the dignity of burial due to his atrocities against his own people.

Despite his ignoble end, the Antichrist will astound the world by rising from the dead, healing from his fatal wound. This miraculous resurrection will evoke awe and admiration among many, further enhancing his mystique and influence. Revelation 13:3-4 vividly portrays this event, with one of his heads appearing mortally wounded but miraculously healed, prompting widespread marvelling and worship of the Beast and the Dragon who empowered him.

However, this apparent triumph will be short-lived, as prophesied in Isaiah 14:25, where the resurrected Antichrist is depicted as meeting his final demise at the hands of the Lord Himself. This serves as a reminder of the transient nature of worldly power and the ultimate sovereignty of God over all things, even the most formidable human rulers.

The details of the Antichrist's resurrection are outlined in Revelation 9, where it is suggested that similar to Christ's resurrection by God the Father, the Antichrist will be raised from the dead by his father, Satan. In verse 1, the fallen "Star," representing Satan, is given the "key to the bottomless pit," indicating his authority over death and resurrection. Subsequently, the Antichrist emerges from the Bottomless Pit, symbolising his resurrection, as described in Revelation 17:8.

This passage emphasises the astonishment and wonder of the earth-dwellers upon witnessing the Antichrist's resurrection. The phrase "was, and is not, and shall ascend out of the Bottomless Pit" conveys the miraculous nature of his return to life. Those whose names are not written in the Book of Life from the foundation of the world will be particularly amazed by this event as they behold the Beast who was once alive, then seemingly ceased to exist, and yet now stands resurrected. The spectacle of a man returning from death will undoubtedly captivate the world's attention, especially given the Antichrist's previous prominence and the shock of his apparent demise.

The resuscitation of the Antichrist, coupled with the healing of his death wound, will lead to widespread amazement and adoration as people marvel at his seemingly supernatural resurrection. This event will cement his status as a figure of immense power and influence, drawing even greater reverence from those who witness his return from the grave.

During the latter half of the Antichrist's reign, the False Prophet, described in Revelation 13:11-16, will emerge as a significant figure. Prophecies suggest that the Antichrist will not remain in Israel for the entirety of this period. Instead, he seems to pivot away from Babylon shortly after the midpoint of the prophesied "week," leaving the False Prophet to wield authority in his absence. This transition marks a shift in focus, with the False Prophet acting as the Antichrist's representative and enforcing the worship of the Beast's image upon the inhabitants of Jerusalem under penalty of death as outlined in Revelation 13:15.

It is important to note the characterisation of the Antichrist as depicted in Habakkuk 2:5, where he is described as "an arrogant man" who extends his dominion far beyond his homeland, relentlessly seeking to gather nations and peoples under his rule. This portrayal aligns with the Antichrist's ambitious and expansionist nature, illustrating his relentless pursuit of power and control on a global scale.

The Antichrist's return to Babylon signifies a pivotal moment in his descent into full defiance against God. Stripped of his religious facade, he now stands as the ultimate adversary of all that bears the name of the Divine. His primary objective is the eradication of anything associated with God, starting with the Jewish people, whom he seeks to completely annihilate. Utilising his full might, he wages war against the Jewish saints, as prophesied in Daniel 7:21 and 8:24, symbolised by the appearance of the "red horse" in Revelation 6:4.

In response, the remnant of the faithful flee to the mountains, echoing the plea for divine intervention found in Psalm 83:1-4. The enemies of God, fueled by hatred and enmity, conspire to eliminate the nation of Israel entirely. The gathering of Jews in Babylon, as foretold in Jeremiah 50:8; 51:6, 45 and Revelation 18:4, becomes a focal point for the Antichrist's vengeance.

However, the Antichrist's reign of terror will not go unchecked indefinitely. In time, heaven will answer the cries of Israel's faithful remnant, unleashing a swift and decisive vengeance upon their ultimate adversary. Yet, as we delve into his last days and final destiny, the full unfolding of these events and the Antichrist's ultimate fate will be explored in the subsequent chapter.

Chapter 10: Demise of the Antichrist

As the end of days draws near, clarity and illumination often emerge regarding prophecies concerning the Antichrist's various phases and stages of his career. This phenomenon aligns with a broader pattern observed in the eschatological timeline. God progressively unveils deeper insights into the events preceding the Second Advent. It's as if God initially provides a general framework, gradually filling in the specific details as the appointed time approaches. Such is the case with the ultimate downfall of the Antichrist.

In these latter days, the Holy Spirit graciously grants us a profound and vivid portrayal of the Son of Perdition's final chapters in his dark saga. With anticipation and apprehension, we examine what has been meticulously recorded for our enlightenment and understanding.

The journey of the Man of Sin indeed leaves us astounded at the depths to which evil can descend. His deceitful machinations, vile duplicity, ruthless violence, and unfathomable impiety stand as a testament to the patience of a God who endures "the vessels of wrath fitted to destruction" with great forbearance. Yet, when we witness the Antichrist openly defying heaven, brazenly rejecting God, and attempting to thwart the arrival of the Lord Jesus on earth, we are left speechless at the unfathomable lengths to which sin will go.

However, amidst this darkness, we recognise that this tumultuous period is the prelude to the dawn of Christ's Day, the Millennium. It serves as a stark backdrop against which the glory of the God-man shines brightly. The downfall of the Antichrist heralds the establishment of the Messianic Kingdom, ushering in an era of unparalleled peace and blessing for all of God's children. As we contemplate this glorious future, our hearts cannot help but overflow with joy and gratitude. Truly, the demise of the Man of Sin marks the dawn of a new age of divine peace and fulfilment.

As we await the glorious Day of Christ's return, we must first endure the darkest hour of His absence. Just as the night is darkest before the dawn, so will the final hour before Christ's return be the most foreboding. This period preceding His coming will be marked by unprecedented calamities and disasters, surpassing any hardship in human history. Daniel foresaw this era of distress, proclaiming, "There shall be a time of trouble, such as never has been since there was a nation till that time" (Daniel 12:1). Jesus Himself alluded to this time, declaring, "For in those days there will be such tribulation as has not been from the beginning of the creation that God created until now, and never will be. And if the Lord had not cut short the days, no human being would be saved. But for the sake of the elect, whom he chose, he shortened the days" (Mark 13:19-20).

According to the Scriptures, this period is referred to as "the hour of trial that is coming on the whole world" (Revelation 3:10). It will be a time of unparalleled wickedness and suffering as God exacts vengeance for the murder of His Son and confronts a world that has long ignored His Word and trampled His commandments. The Antichrist will emerge as one of the instruments of God's judgment, wielding His righteous indignation like a rod (Isaiah 10:5).

Humanity's rejection of the love of God's truth sets the stage for the Antichrist's deception, as described in Scripture. God, in response, allows a strong delusion to take hold, leading people to believe the Devil's lies. This delusion finds fertile ground among those who derive pleasure from unrighteousness as they embrace falsehood over the truth. Israel, having rejected the true Messiah who came in His Father's name, will instead welcome the Antichrist, who comes in his own name. Thus, the Lawless One will deceive many, prospering for a time and appearing to challenge God's authority.

However, God's allowance of the Antichrist's reign serves a purpose, as He works through him to fulfil His divine plan. Yet, there are limits set by God to the Antichrist's dominion, akin to how God established the boundaries of the sea. When these limits are reached, the Antichrist will find himself powerless to deviate from God's ultimate purpose, akin to a worm beneath an elephant's foot. This divine control over the Antichrist's actions will become evident as we continue exploring the prophecy's unfolding.

The anguish of the Jewish people as they face the Antichrist's assaults is poignantly captured in Psalm 74:1-11. They cry out to God in despair, questioning why He seems to have abandoned them in their time of need. They recount the desecration of their sanctuary and the destruction wrought by their enemies, lamenting the absence of miraculous signs and prophets among them. Their plea for God's intervention is filled with desperation, longing for Him to arise and defend His people against their adversaries.

This moment of despair aligns with the prophecy of Amos 8, where Yahweh declares His judgment upon the prideful nation of Jacob. The land trembles as it experiences upheaval, and mourning envelops its inhabitants. Yahweh promises to turn their feasts into mourning and their songs into lamentation, bringing a profound sense of loss and grief. A spiritual famine descends upon the land, not for bread or water, but for the word of Yahweh. People search vain for His word, but it remains elusive, leading to widespread spiritual thirst and fainting among the youth.

This prophecy paints a grim picture of the spiritual and emotional turmoil that grips the land as the Antichrist's reign brings devastation and despair. Yet, amidst the darkness, there remains hope for the eventual restoration and redemption promised by God to His people.

The assurance of God's protection and deliverance for His people shines brightly amidst the darkness of persecution and despair. In Isaiah 10:24-25, Yahweh, the Lord of Armies, encourages His people not to fear the Assyrian, representing the Antichrist, even as he wields his power against them. God promises that His indignation against His people will soon be accomplished, and His anger will be directed towards the destruction of their oppressors. This assurance echoes throughout Scripture, reaffirming God's faithfulness to His covenant with Israel.

As the Antichrist turns his aggression towards Israel, his days are indeed numbered, for God fiercely guards His chosen nation as the apple of His eye (Zechariah 2:8). Isaiah 10:26 declares that God has prepared a scourge for him, indicating the swift and decisive judgment awaiting the Antichrist for his atrocities against God's people.

Furthermore, Daniel 11:40 foretells a confrontation between the Antichrist and opposing forces, symbolised by the king of the south and the king of the north. These powers will come against the Antichrist like a whirlwind, with great military might and overwhelming force. Despite the Antichrist's temporary reign of terror, God's ultimate victory and deliverance for His people are assured.

These prophecies serve as a beacon of hope for the faithful remnant of Israel and all who trust in God's promises. They remind us that God is sovereign over the affairs of nations and that His purposes will ultimately prevail, bringing justice, deliverance, and redemption to His people.

In the intricate tapestry of biblical prophecy, the roles and movements of nations are depicted with remarkable detail and symbolism. In

Daniel 11:41, Egypt emerges as the southern monarch who takes decisive action against the Antichrist, the king of the north, symbolising Assyria. This aggression triggers a swift and tumultuous response from the Antichrist, who mobilises his formidable forces from Babylon, his seat of power, towards Egypt like a whirlwind of destruction.

The imagery of the Antichrist's march, likened to a rushing mountain stream, vividly portrays his military campaign's speed and overwhelming force as it sweeps over the land, leaving devastation in its wake. Along the way, the Antichrist's forces also traverse through Israel, a nation soon to be renowned for its glory, where their impact will undoubtedly be felt. However, the specifics are not detailed in the prophecy.

Interestingly, certain regions and peoples are spared from his wrath amidst the chaos and upheaval of the Antichrist's conquests. Edom, Moab, and the descendants of Ammon are singled out as escaping his hand. This exemption is rooted in their collaboration with the Antichrist in conspiring against God's people, as outlined in Psalm 83. When the Antichrist's campaign to eradicate the Jewish people is launched, these nations align themselves with his cause, earning them favour and protection from his aggression.

Thus, in biblical prophecy's intricate geopolitical manoeuvring foretold, we see the interplay between divine judgment, human agency, and God's redemptive plan unfolding. The sparing of certain nations amidst the Antichrist's onslaught serves as a sobering reminder of the complexities and consequences of aligning oneself with the forces of darkness, as well as the ultimate triumph of God's righteousness and justice.

Indeed, the sparing of Edom, Moab, and the children of Ammon from the Antichrist's immediate wrath carries both a human and divine dimension. Humanly, their collaboration with the Antichrist in opposing God's people earns them a temporary reprieve from his aggression. However, divinely, their sparing serves as a prelude to their eventual judgment by God.

Ancient prophecies, such as those uttered by the pagan prophet Balaam, foretell the eventual demise of these nations at the hands of the coming Messiah. The rise of a sceptre out of Israel signifies the authority and dominion of the Messiah, who will bring judgment upon Moab and the offspring of Sheth, referring to Edom. These events are slated to occur at the commencement of the millennial reign when Israel will assert its dominance over these territories.

Moreover, the Antichrist's conquest extends beyond Egypt, as he gains control over the treasures of gold, silver, and precious resources within the land. The nations of Libya and Ethiopia, as allies of Egypt, were also brought under his dominion, further consolidating his power and influence in the region. His swift and decisive actions crush any opposition and reinforce his image of invincibility and dominance.

However, despite his temporary successes and apparent supremacy, the Antichrist's defiance of divine authority cannot go unchecked indefinitely. The divine hand of judgment looms over him, and his days of reckoning draw near. As history unfolds according to the divine plan, the Antichrist's reign of terror will eventually end, paving the way for establishing God's eternal kingdom of righteousness and peace.

The prophecy in Daniel 11:44 foretells troubling reports that will disturb the Antichrist, prompting him to unleash his wrath in a campaign of destruction. These reports likely originate from the east and the north, signalling potential threats or challenges to his authority. In response, the Antichrist will mobilise his forces with great fury, seeking to annihilate many and assert his dominance.

Jeremiah 51 provides vivid imagery of the impending judgment upon Babylon, the capital of the Antichrist's domain. The kings of Ararat, Minni, and Ashkenaz are depicted as besieging and seizing one end of the city, a sign of the growing opposition to Babylon's tyranny. This may be fueled by Egypt's insubordination, further escalating regional tensions.

God's condemnation of Babylon is unequivocal, portraying it as a destroying mountain that will be brought low and made desolate forever. The imagery of Babylon as a burned mountain with no cornerstone or foundation stone underscores the completeness of its destruction. The call to "prepare the nations against her" and the imagery of trembling and pain indicate the inevitability of Babylon's downfall and the fulfilment of God's purposes.

The once mighty men of Babylon are depicted as powerless, their strength depleted, and their defences breached. The destruction of their dwelling places and the breaking of their bars symbolise the collapse of Babylon's formidable defences and the onset of its demise. As the prophetic warnings are sounded and the nations gather against Babylon, the stage is set for the final judgment and the ultimate fulfilment of God's divine plan.

The distressing news of Babylon's partial destruction reaches the ears of its king, who is then in Egypt, provoking him to great rage and a fervent desire for retaliation. This reaction is described in Daniel 11:44 as the king's determination to demolish and destroy many in his path. As he returns to his capital, messengers relay the dire situation to him, informing him of the city's siege and the impending threat to its existence.

Jeremiah 51 vividly portrays the impending judgment upon Babylon, likening it to a threshing floor ready for harvest. The daughter of Babylon, representing the city itself, is depicted as being ripe for destruction, with the time of her reckoning drawing near. God's command for His people to flee Babylon's midst echoes His warning to escape the coming wrath, urging them to save their souls from the fierce anger of the Lord.

Jeremiah 51 and Revelation 18 depict Babylon's downfall, emphasising the swift and decisive judgment awaiting the city. These passages serve as a sobering reminder of the consequences of rebellion against God and the inevitable fate of those who oppose His righteous authority.

The Antichrist's wrath upon witnessing Babylon's destruction will be unparalleled. Driven by fury and resentment towards God, he will redirect his focus towards Israel, unleashing his formidable army upon the sacred land. Yet, even in his blinded rage, God's sovereign hand guides the Antichrist and his followers, using them as instruments of judgment upon Israel and ultimately leading them to their own tragic demise.

Habakkuk vividly portrays the ruthless and swift nature of the Chaldeans, symbolising the Antichrist and his armies as they sweep across the land with cruelty and haste. Their advance is characterised by unparalleled speed and ferocity likened to swift predators and soaring eagles. Their thirst for violence knows no bounds, and they will stop at nothing to conquer and dominate. This onslaught will be so devastating that Zechariah prophesies a grim outcome, with two-thirds of the land's inhabitants perishing in the onslaught.

The imagery painted by these prophets underscores the severity of the Antichrist's assault on Israel and the harrowing consequences it will bring upon its people. Yet, amidst the darkness and destruction, there remains a glimmer of hope as God's divine plan unfolds, ultimately leading to the redemption and restoration of His chosen people.

In the ninth chapter of Isaiah's prophecy, a vivid narrative unfolds, detailing the relentless advance of the Antichrist's forces through various locations, each falling under the shadow of impending doom. From Aiath to Migron and then Mickmash, the Antichrist's armies march with swift determination, setting up their camps and preparing for battle. The once bustling towns like Ramah and Geba now tremble in fear as the ominous presence of the enemy looms closer. Even the fortified city of Nob, though temporarily spared, serves as a mere waypoint for the Antichrist's impending assault on Jerusalem.

As the night descends upon the land, the Antichrist stands atop the heights of Nob, overlooking the majestic city of Jerusalem spread out before him. With a gesture of defiance, he shakes his hand against the mount of the daughter of Zion, symbolising his brazen challenge to the authority of God and His chosen people. The mention of placing the tabernacles of his palace "between the seas on the goodly holy mountain" in Daniel 11:45 further emphasises the Antichrist's audacious ambition to establish his dominion over Jerusalem, the heart of God's kingdom on earth.

The scene at Armageddon is one of anticipation and preparation for the final, climactic battle between the forces of good and evil. Joel's prophetic words ring out, calling the Gentiles to arms and urging them to ready themselves for combat. Ploughshares are transformed into swords, and hooks are pruned into spears, as even the weakest find newfound strength in the face of the impending conflict.

The heathen are summoned to assemble, and the Lord's mighty ones are invoked to descend upon the valley of Jehoshaphat, where divine judgment will be rendered upon the nations. The imagery evokes a sense of urgency as the sickle is readied for the harvest, symbolising the gathering of the wicked for their final reckoning.

Multitudes gather in the valley of decision, where the fate of nations hangs in the balance. In this pivotal moment, the Lord's day draws near, signalling the culmination of history and the establishment of His righteous reign over all creation.

Micah's prophetic vision unveils the gathering of many nations against Zion, oblivious to the divine purposes unfolding before them. Despite their intent to defile and conquer, they are mere pawns in the hands of the Almighty, who will ultimately gather them like sheaves upon the threshing floor.

The battleground shifts to the vicinity of Jerusalem, where the forces of the Antichrist, symbolising God's righteous judgment, deliver the final blow upon the city before the long-awaited appearance of the Deliverer. In this dramatic moment, God addresses Assyria, designating it as the instrument of His wrath and the staff of His displeasure. Assyria is tasked with confronting a hypocritical nation, charged with the plundering and subjugation of those who have incurred God's righteous anger, trampling them down like street filth in fulfilment of divine justice.

Despite the Antichrist's arrogance and delusions of grandeur, divine providence ultimately orchestrates his actions. Though his intentions may not align with God's will, his heart is set on causing harm and dominating many nations. He boasts of his conquests, equating his reign over various cities with that of mighty kings.

In his pride, he challenges the power of God, questioning whether his dominion over earthly kingdoms is akin to the triumphs of ancient rulers. Yet, just as God's hand brought down the kingdoms of idolatrous nations in the past, the Antichrist presumes he can replicate this feat with Jerusalem and its idols.

However, in the grand tapestry of divine sovereignty, the Antichrist unwittingly serves as an instrument of the Lord's purpose. Just as Moses wielded the rod that transformed into a serpent, God will manipulate the actions of the Antichrist, using him to fulfil His predetermined counsels and bring about the culmination of His divine plan.

Once again, the Antichrist, symbolised as the Beast, appears to achieve a measure of success. The prophetic words of Jehovah foretell a grim reality: all nations will gather against Jerusalem for war, resulting in the city's capture, homes being plundered, women subjected to violence, and a portion of the population taken into captivity, while the rest remain in the besieged city (Zechariah 14:2).

In their defiance against the Lord and His anointed, the world's kings unite and conspire to break free from what they perceive as constraints imposed upon them. Their rebellion mirrors the sentiments expressed in the psalmist's lament, where the nations rage and the people devise futile schemes against the divine order (Psalm 2:2, 3). Despite their arrogance and defiance, they fail to recognise the futility of their endeavours in the face of divine sovereignty.

In the climactic moment, the grandeur of the heavens unfolds as the King of kings and Lord of lords emerges, seated upon a majestic white horse, His eyes ablaze like fire (Revelation 19:11, 12). Accompanied by the heavenly host, arrayed in dazzling white and mounted on white horses, He leads His divine army into the fray (Revelation 19:14).

Instead of bowing in reverence to this awe-inspiring manifestation of divine authority, the Beast and the rulers of the earth, in a brazen display of defiance, muster their forces to wage war against the One seated on the horse and His celestial army (Revelation 19:19). It is a moment reminiscent of ancient conflicts, where nations clashed on the battlefield under the sovereign hand of God (Zechariah 14:3).

Yet, as the battle commences, it quickly becomes evident that this is no ordinary confrontation. The opposition's defiance is swiftly quelled, their movements arrested, and their resistance shattered in the face of divine supremacy. The outcome of the conflict is certain from the moment it begins – the victory belongs unequivocally to the Lord of hosts.

The Scriptures vividly document the downfall of numerous wicked figures throughout history, each meeting their end in various ways. Some were swallowed by the depths of the sea, others consumed by raging flames; some were swallowed by the earth's gaping maw, while others were afflicted with devastating plagues. Some faced ignominious slaughter, others met their demise at the end of a hangman's noose; some were torn apart by ravenous beasts, and others were consumed by the relentless jaws of worms. However, amidst these diverse fates, none can compare to the destiny reserved for the Man of Sin, the epitome of evil, who shall meet his end at the luminous revelation of the Lord Jesus Christ.

His fate, as foretold in the prophetic scriptures, is unparalleled in its awe-inspiring finality. With righteousness, the Lord shall judge the poor and reprove with equity for the meek of the earth. Yet, with the divine authority of His word, He shall strike the earth, and with the breath of His lips, He shall utterly destroy the Wicked One (Isaiah 11:14).

The rise of this sinister figure, characterised by his cunning deceit and prideful ambition, will ultimately lead to his downfall. Despite his schemes to manipulate and deceive, he shall ultimately be shattered without human intervention, a fate often associated with supernatural intervention (Daniel 8:25).

His hubris, manifested in establishing his palace between the seas upon the majestic holy mountain, will be his undoing. Despite his lofty aspirations, he shall come to a sudden and irreversible end, forsaken by all (Daniel 11:45).

Paul prophesies the Wicked One's demise in his epistle to the Thessalonians, foretelling his exposure and ultimate destruction by the radiant glory of the Lord's appearance (2 Thessalonians 2:8).

In the apocalyptic vision of Revelation, the Beast and the False Prophet, symbols of the Antichrist and his deceiver, meet their end in a lake of fire and brimstone, cast alive into eternal torment for their deception and blasphemy (Revelation 19:20).

The imagery of Tophet, ordained for the king's judgment, is a potent reminder of the divine wrath awaiting the wicked. Its depths, filled with fire and brimstone, symbolise the unquenchable fury of the Lord's judgment upon the unrepentant (Isaiah 30:33).

The fate awaiting the Antichrist's followers is as dreadful as their leader's. In the apocalyptic vision of Revelation, the Devil, who deceived them, is cast into the lake of fire and brimstone, along with the Beast and the False Prophet. They shall endure torment day and night, forever and ever (Revelation 20:10).

Zechariah's prophecy foretold the divine retribution upon those who opposed Jerusalem. The Lord will afflict them with a grievous plague, causing their flesh to waste away. At the same time, they stand, their eyes to consume in their sockets, and their tongues to consume in their mouths (Zechariah 14:12). Such suffering will provoke a great panic among them, leading to desperate acts of violence as they turn against one another (Zechariah 14:13).

The scene depicted in Revelation 19:21 further emphasises the swift and decisive judgment upon the Antichrist's followers. They are slain by the sword that proceeds from the mouth of the victorious Rider on the white horse, symbolising the power of divine judgment. Their flesh becomes food for the birds of the air, highlighting the utter defeat and destruction of those who opposed the Lord's reign (Revelation 19:21).

Bibliography

Ryrie, Charles C. (1969). *The Basis of the Premillennial Faith.* Moody Press.

Walvoord, John F. (1957). *The Millennial Kingdom.* Zondervan.

Pentecost, J. Dwight. (1958). *Things to Come: A Study in Biblical Eschatology.* Zondervan.

Ladd, George Eldon. (1956). *The Blessed Hope: A Biblical Study of the Second Advent and the Rapture.* William B. Eerdmans Publishing Company.

Hitchcock, Mark. (2011). *The End: A Complete Overview of Bible Prophecy and the End of Days.* Tyndale House Publishers.

Fruchtenbaum, Arnold G. (2004). *Footsteps of the Messiah.* Ariel Ministries.

Lindsey, Hal. (1970). *The Late Great Planet Earth.* Zondervan.

Jenkins, Jerry B., and Tim LaHaye. (2005). *The Rapture: In the Twinkling of an Eye / Countdown to the Earth's Last Days.* Tyndale House Publishers.

Ice, Thomas, and Timothy J. Demy. (2011). *The Return: A Novel of the Rapture.* B&H Books.

www.ingramcontent.com/pod-product-compliance
Lightning Source LLC
Chambersburg PA
CBHW031738150726
47989CB00006B/2511